To Leti from Grama

God and me

This book belongs to

....

God and me

365 daily devotions

Penny Boshoff

Authentic

For my mother, Tricia Beaumont, whose faith and love inspired me, and without whom this book would not exist. **Joanna Bicknell**

09 08 07 06 05 04   6 5 4 3 2 1
Published by Authentic Media
129 Mobilization Drive, Waynesboro, GA 30830 USA
authenticusa@stl.org

ISBN 1932805-22-2
Printed and bound in Singapore.

make
believe
ideas

Photographer: Andy Snaith
Designers: Cameron Emerson-Elliott, Bruce Wallace
Editor: Sarah Phillips
Project manager: Dania Vize
American consultant: Claudia Volkman
make believe ideas would like to thank Jenny Hyatt and Su Box for editorial input, and Leena Lane for help with the writing.

Contents

A new day

It's a new day! Time to have a good stretch and get dressed, time for breakfast, time to talk to God. As you put on your clothes, thank God for the new day and tell him what you are going to do. Ask him to help you and take care of you all through the day.

PRAYER FOR TODAY
Thanks for this new day, God, a fun day, a play day, a "busy things to do" day, Help me all the way, God. Be with me today. Amen.

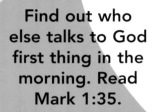

Find out who else talks to God first thing in the morning. Read Mark 1:35.

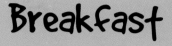
Breakfast

When I wake up, I'm hungry and ready for my breakfast, lunch and dinner. I like cereal and peanut butter on toast. But some people like eggs and bacon, waffles and syrup, or yogurt and fruit. God has given us lots of delicious food to start our day. Let's remember to thank him.

PRAYER FOR TODAY
Dear God, thank you for breakfast food. I like

....

best for my breakfast.
Amen.

We can thank God for our food at breakfast, lunch, and dinner, just as Jesus did. See Luke 9:16.

Grumpy or jumpy?

Are you grumpy or jumpy in the morning? It's easy to be jumpy on a sunny morning and grumpy on a cold, rainy day. But whether it is sunny or rainy, it's a day made by God. He gives us each new day so we can get to know him better. What sort of day is it today?

PRAYER FOR TODAY
Thank you for giving me today, God. I want to learn more about you and get to know you better.
Amen.

God makes each new day. And every day God shows us he loves us. Read Lamentations 3:22–24.

Helping others

Jesus wants us to be helpful. There are lots of ways we can help at home and at school. Tom is helping his mom by putting his baby sister's hat on for her. You might help someone at school to put on their shoes or button their coat. How else could you help your brother, sister, or friends?

Jesus tells a story about a man who helps someone else in Luke 10:25–37.

Writing

Writing is fun but it can be difficult at first. Some letters are tricky to write so the children are concentrating very hard. Amy is trying to write the letter "a," Chloe is writing a story, and Matthew has written his name. Writing takes lots of practice! What do you like to write?

PRAYER FOR TODAY
Tell Jesus about the things you write. Dear Jesus, I can write

....

Please help me to write clearly. Amen.

Luke tells us all about Jesus' life, but first he writes something very important. What is it? See Luke 1:1–4.

Being naughty

Jen is having a bad day! There are some days when no matter how hard we try, we end up doing something wrong. The good news is that however naughty we have been and whatever we have done wrong, God always forgives us.

PRAYER FOR TODAY
Dear God, I'm sorry for the wrong things I've done today. Thank you for forgiving me. You're great! Amen.

God welcomes us and forgives us just like the father in Jesus' story. Read Luke 15:11–24.

comforting...

When you are sad, who makes you feel better? Isn't it great that God gives us moms and dads, grandmas and grandpas, and brothers and sisters to comfort us when we are sad? And even though we cannot see God, he is always there to help us, too.

PRAYER FOR TODAY
Dear God, it's good to know that you are always with me. Thank you especially for

....,

who makes me feel better. Amen.

The Bible tells us that God comforts us so that we can comfort other people. See 2 Corinthians 1:3–4.

. . . and Cheering

God is pleased when we help people who are sad. When your friends are sad, what do you do to make them feel better? Maybe you put your arm around them, give them a hug, smile at them, share your toys, play their favorite game, or tell them a joke. There are so many ways to show you care!

PRAYER FOR TODAY
When my friends are lonely, worried, or sad, Lord Jesus, show me the way to make them feel glad. Amen.

In today's Bible story, Ruth helps her friend Naomi when she is very sad. Look at Ruth 1:16–18.

Helpful hair

Chloe's hair looks pretty but it is also very useful. In the cold of winter, Chloe's hair helps to keep her head warm. In the hot summer weather, her hair stops her head from getting sunburned. Next time you look in the mirror, thank God for giving you such useful hair!

PRAYER FOR TODAY
Hair is a wonderful thing, God! Thank you for my hair. Amen.

The woman in today's story uses her hair as a towel! Read John 12:1–8.

Hands to touch

God designed our hands so that we can touch and feel. If you shut your eyes and touch with your hands, you will be able to tell if something is prickly or furry, rough or smooth, hard or soft. Our hands can even feel if something is hot or cold. If you were to stroke these animals, what would they feel like?

PRAYER FOR TODAY
Creator God, it's amazing what my hands can tell me! Thank you for making my hands so well.
Amen.

In today's story, Isaac needs his hands to touch and feel things because he is blind. See Genesis 27:21–27.

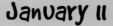

Reading

Emily is learning to read. She knows all her letters and sounds. Now she is beginning to recognize words. Learning to read is fun! Emily wants to be able to read the stories about Jesus by herself, just like her big sister does.

PRAYER FOR TODAY
Thank you, God, for books and stories. Please help me with my reading so I can read by myself.
Amen

Today's Bible verses tell why it's important to read God's word. Read 2 Timothy 3:16–17.

Growing and learning

Growing up is fun! We get older and bigger and we learn to do new things. What can you do now that you couldn't do when you were little? Can you ride a bike, catch a ball, or read a book? God wants us to become more like Jesus as we grow up. Jesus loved God and was kind and good to others.

PRAYER FOR TODAY
Help me, Jesus, to grow more like you, loving God and loving others, too.
Amen.

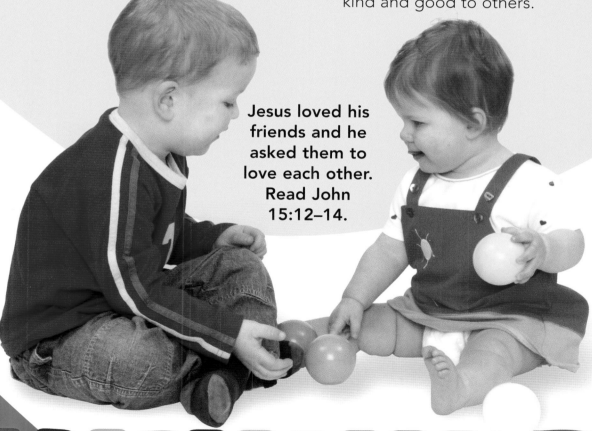

Jesus loved his friends and he asked them to love each other. Read John 15:12–14.

Talking on the phone

When Milly talks to her grandma on the phone, she can't see her but she knows it is Grandma listening and talking to her. It's like that when we pray. We can't see God but the Bible tells us that when we talk to God, he listens very carefully to us. We can talk to him about anything and everything!

PRAYER FOR TODAY
Dear God, it's great that I can tell you anything. Thank you for always listening to me. Help me listen to you, too. Amen.

Jesus wants us to talk to our Father in heaven. See Matthew 6:6–15.

A princess!

Alice has found some dress-up clothes at nursery school to make her look like a princess. It's fun pretending to be a princess or superman! Do you like dressing up? Who do you pretend to be – a king, a fairy, a fireman, or someone else?

PRAYER FOR TODAY
Dear God, I like dressing up. I like being

....

the best.
Amen.

There is a Bible story about a real princess. She was beautiful, but she was also very brave. You can find her story in Esther.

Rain! Rain! Rain!

When it rains, Emily can't wait to go out to play. Sometimes the rain is warm, sometimes it's cold. Raindrops can be tiny, like a gentle cloud, or great big drops that splash on your hands and face. That's the rain Emily likes the best. She's glad God made the rain!

PRAYER FOR TODAY
Dear God, thank you for sending rain. On rainy days, I like to

....
Amen.

Today's story is about a land where it hasn't rained for three years. Read 1 Kings 18:1–2, 41–46.

Rain for the grass

Do you like the rain? Or do you like sunshine every day? Imagine what would happen if it never rained! The grass wouldn't grow. The cows would have nothing to eat. They wouldn't make any milk and we wouldn't have cheese for pizza, ice cream, or milkshakes! What a good thing God sends rain to make the grass grow!

PRAYER FOR TODAY
Dear God, you take care of everything you have made. Thank you for sending rain to make the grass grow. Amen.

Psalm 147:7–8 tells us that God sends the rain. What does it say we should do?

Being patient

We love our brothers and sisters but sometimes they annoy us! God understands that we get crabby. He wants us to learn to be kind, gentle, and patient. So the next time your brother or sister is annoying you, ask God to help you to be loving towards them.

PRAYER FOR TODAY
Dear God, you are kind and good. You are gentle and patient with me. Help me to be like you.
Amen.

God helps us to grow more like him. See Galatians 5:22–23.

A bad mood

When I'm in a bad mood, I want to be left alone. When my friend is in a bad mood, she shouts a lot. What do you do when you are in a bad mood? God knows when we are grumpy and he still loves us. He is always ready to listen to us.

PRAYER FOR TODAY
Dear God, help me to remember that I can always talk to you. Thank you for wanting to listen to me even when I'm in a bad mood. Amen.

The people who wrote the songs and prayers of the Psalms told God exactly how they felt. Read Psalm 40:12–15.

Ears

Close your eyes and listen very carefully. What different sounds can you hear? God gives us ears so that we can hear VERY LOUD noises and tiny, quiet noises. He knows that we need ears to listen to our favorite music and to each other. Isn't is great that God invented ears?

PRAYER FOR TODAY
Thank you, God, for my two ears.Thank you, God, that I can hear. Amen.

The man in today's story cannot hear or talk. Find out what happens to him in Mark 7:31–38.

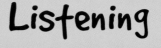

Listening

When the TV is on very loud, Chloe can't hear what her mom is saying. But sometimes Chloe can hear exactly what her mom says but she doesn't want to listen. God wants us to listen to our parents and do what they ask us, even when they say, "Pick up your toys," or "Time for bed!"

PRAYER FOR TODAY

Dear God, some days I don't want to listen to my mom and dad. I'm sorry. Please help me to listen carefully to them. Amen.

Ephesians 6:1–3 tells us to listen to our moms and our dads and do what they tell us.

Party time

George is helping his mom with the food for his sister's party. Look at his huge plate of sweets – they look delicious! George isn't the only one getting ready for a party. Did you know that God is planning a big party, too? His party will be in heaven and he wants us to be there. Won't that be fun?

PRAYER FOR TODAY
Thank you, God, for inviting me to your party in heaven. I really want to come! Amen.

There will be lots of people at God's party. Where will they all come from? Read Luke 13:29–30 to find out.

Your brain

God has given you a brain. It is so important, you can't live without it. It tells your body what to do, so you can run, eat, and brush your teeth. It helps you to work out what to say before you say it. You use it to remember what you've done today and to think about what you want to do tomorrow. Isn't that amazing?

PRAYER FOR TODAY
Dear God, thank you for my brain. Help me to use it well. Amen.

Other people may not know what you are thinking, but God does! See Psalm 139:1–2.

Nighttime

Do you ever feel scared of the dark? You don't need to be because nighttime was God's idea. He made the days for us to learn and grow and the nights for us to rest our bodies. In fact, darkness helps our bodies to go to sleep. Isn't that wonderful?

PRAYER FOR TODAY

Dear God, who made
the quiet, dark night,
please keep me safe
'til morning's light.
Amen.

Read about God creating nighttime in Genesis 1:3–5.

Counting Stars

Can you count the stars in the sky? How many do you think there are? When God made the universe, he filled it with millions and millions of stars. Did you know that there are more stars than there are grains of sand on all the beaches of the world? How awesome of God to make such an enormous universe for all those stars!

PRAYER FOR TODAY
God, you're really great at imagining and making things. I love all the stars you made! Amen.

God tells Abraham to go out and count the stars. Find out what happens in Genesis 15:4–6.

A helping hand

It's fun helping our friends. We help them with things they can't do by themselves and they help us, too. Sophie can't braid her own hair so Milly is doing it for her. God is pleased when we help our friends because it shows that we love them. Try to think of different ways you could help your friends!

PRAYER FOR TODAY
Hello God, my friend helps me

to...
And I help him/her to

....
Amen.

Read what the Bible says about helping each other in Hebrews 10:24.

Making faces

Jen is making a very funny face! Making faces to make people laugh can be fun but making faces to be rude is not kind at all. Sometimes Jen and her friends call each other names, too. They do it for fun, but it's easy to hurt someone's feelings. What do you think Jesus would want them to do?

PRAYER FOR TODAY
Dear God, when my friends and I are having fun, help us to speak kindly to each other. Amen.

Read Ephesians 4:29 to find out how God wants us to speak to each other.

Animals galore!

How many different animals can you think of? God made all sorts of animals. He made tall ones and tiny ones, smooth ones and wrinkly ones, scaly ones and furry ones. God has thought of everything!

PRAYER FOR TODAY

You're great, God! I'm glad you made so many different animals. My favorite animal is

....

Amen.

Read Genesis 1:20–25 to find out what God thinks about the animals he made.

Caring for animals

This is Puff, George's rabbit. Isn't she wonderful? Wouldn't you like to stroke her long, soft fur? I know I would. George doesn't want to hurt Puff, so he is stroking her very gently. God is really pleased when we are kind to the animals he made.

PRAYER FOR TODAY
Dear God, thank you for making so many different animals for us to care for and enjoy. I want to love them, too. Please help me to be kind and gentle to my pets. Amen.

Today's Bible story is about a sheep that got lost. Find it in Luke 15:3–7.

Fishing

George is using a toy rod to catch his toy fish. But to catch real fish, you need to use big nets! Fishermen go far out to sea in boats and catch the fish in huge nets. The fishermen have to be fit, strong, and brave because it can be dangerous out on the ocean in stormy weather.

PRAYER FOR TODAY

Dear God, please keep all fishermen safe as they work far out at sea to bring us fish to eat. Amen.

Read about Jesus' fishermen friends in Luke 5:1–11.

Feeling lonely

Do you sometimes feel lonely. Maybe it's when you are in bed at night. Or maybe you feel lonely in a busy playground, when no one wants to play your games. But wherever you are, in quiet places or noisy places, God is always with you. He loves you, and he will never leave you on your own.

PRAYER FOR TODAY
Dear God,
you never leave me on my own,
you're with me night and day,
I think of you, and know you're near,
when no one wants to play.
Amen.

God has promised he will never leave us. See Hebrews 13:5.

New Clothes

Josh has grown so quickly that his T-shirts are all too short and too tight. So his mom has bought him this new T-shirt. Josh is very pleased with it. He is going to give his favorite old T-shirt to his little brother. What do you do with the clothes that you have outgrown?

PRAYER FOR TODAY

Dear God, thank you for all my clothes. Please take care of people who don't have many clothes to wear.
Amen.

Samuel's mom makes clothes for him as he grows bigger.
Read 1 Samuel 2:18–19.

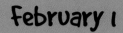
Growing

When we grow, we get taller and bigger. How do you know if you have grown? Sometimes your clothes tell you! When your jeans feel tight around the middle and seem to be getting shorter – you have grown! Sometimes you discover you can do things you couldn't do before – like reaching the light switch. It's fun growing bigger!

PRAYER FOR TODAY
I'm growing and I'm getting bigger every single day.
Jesus, help me grow to be like you in every way.
Amen.

The Bible tells us about Jesus growing bigger. See Luke 2:40–52.

Being ill

It is miserable being ill. When you have a sore tummy or have hurt yourself, what makes you feel better? Medicines, bandages, and lotions help our body to get better. Hugs and gentle care from our moms and dads help us to feel better, too!

PRAYER FOR TODAY
Dear God, I know you care for me when I'm not well.
Thank you for

....,
which makes me feel much better.
Amen.

Jesus tells a story about a man who is hurt. Find out who takes care of him. Read Luke 10:30–35.

wash your hands!

Wash and rub, clean and scrub! It's a good thing God gave us water because we need to wash our hands lots of times every day. We wash them before we eat and after we have been to the bathroom. We wash our hands to clean away dirt and germs that could make us ill. Can you think of other times when you need to wash your hands?

PRAYER FOR TODAY
Dear God, help me to understand how important it is to keep my hands clean. Amen.

Naaman has to wash lots of times. Read his story in 2 Kings 5:1–14 and find out why!

Singing

I love singing! I like to sing on my own, but it's much more fun singing with my friends. We sing LOUD songs and quiet songs. We like clapping, stomping, and dancing songs. We especially like "thank you" songs. We thank God for loving us so much. Do you know any "thank you" songs?

PRAYER FOR TODAY
I'll sing "thank you,"
I will praise you,
for your love for me.
I'll sing my song,
'cause I belong
to you, my God and king.
Amen.

Psalm 117 is a song telling everybody in the world to thank God for his love!

Praise!

From Alaska to Australia, from Chile to China, from Nigeria to Norway, men and women, boys and girls sing songs of praise to God, who made us all. The whole world and everyone in it belongs to him. He loves and cares for us all. What a wonderful God we have!

PRAYER FOR TODAY

It's amazing that you love and care for everybody in the world. I'm glad I belong to you. You're great, God!
Amen.

Psalm 86:8–10 is a song about how powerful and wonderful God is. There is no one like him!

Bath and bubbles

It's bath time! Jo loves baths. He plays with his toys and splashes. And he washes all over, too! What do you do in the bath? Do you have a favorite toy to play with? Do like to have lots of bubbles in your bath or none at all?

PRAYER FOR TODAY
Tell God what you like best about bath time.
Dear God, thank you for warm water. At bath time, I like to

....

Amen.

Peter once asked Jesus to give him a bath! Find out why in John 13:2–17.

A scared fairy!

Rachel wants to be a fairy in her school concert, but she knows that all the moms and dads will be there. She is feeling a little bit scared. Have you ever had to dance or sing in front of lots of people? How did you feel? When we feel nervous or scared, we can ask God to help us to be brave.

PRAYER FOR TODAY

Dear God, I get nervous or scared when

....

Please help me to be brave.
Amen.

Find out what God says when Joshua is feeling scared. See Joshua 1:5–9.

Making friends

It's fun making friends. We meet new friends in all sorts of places – at school, at church, at play groups. Where did you meet your friends? Li's family has just moved to the town where Max lives. Li is a little shy, but I think he and Max will be good friends. They both love playing football!

> **PRAYER FOR TODAY**
> Dear God, I like my friends. Please help me to be friendly to new people. And please help me when I feel shy. Amen.

In today's story, Paul has moved to a new town. Find out who makes friends with him. See Acts 16:11–15.

Keeping promises

Li is starting at Max's school soon. Max has promised to play with Li at playtime. Max already has lots of other friends at school. Do you think he will keep his promise? I think he will! Li will be happy and God will be pleased with Max. God always keeps his promises and he wants us to keep our promises, too.

PRAYER FOR TODAY

Lord, you keep your promises,
help me to keep mine, too,
keep me true to what I say,
I want to be like you!
Amen.

Psalm 145:13 tells us that God always keeps his promises.

Sharing toys

Olivia likes going to Trent's house. Trent is very good at sharing his toys. They both like drawing on the big blackboard. What do you like to doing when your friends come over to play? God shares his whole world with us so he is always pleased when we share our home and our toys with others.

PRAYER FOR TODAY
Thank you, God, for my home and my toys. Help me to share them with my friends.
Amen.

The woman in 2 Kings 4:8–17 is good at sharing. Who does she share with?

Useful hands

What are Trent and Olivia doing with their hands? I'm glad God gave us hands because we use them to do lots of things – painting, drawing, cutting, and pasting. Can you think of other things you do with your hands?

PRAYER FOR TODAY
Tell God what you like doing with your hands. Dear God, it's great you gave me hands! I like using my hands to

....

Amen.

Read Jeremiah 18:1–4. What is the person in today's story doing with his hands?

Going home

It's time to go home! Now that Katie is at school she has to put on her own shoes and coat. Then she runs outside to show her mom what she has made at school today. It's nice to go home after a busy day. Who comes to pick you up from school? Do you talk about your day, just like Katie?

PRAYER FOR TODAY
Dear God, I'm glad I don't go home alone. Thank you for

....,
who is always there
to pick me up.
Amen.

In today's story, Mary and Joseph find Jesus and take him safely home. See Luke 2:41–52.

Swimming

Some people love swimming, splashing, jumping, and diving into the water. But other people hate it! They don't like getting water in their eyes. They don't like being in deep water or being splashed. God knows how you feel about swimming. He knows what you love and what you hate. He is there to help you whenever you are scared.

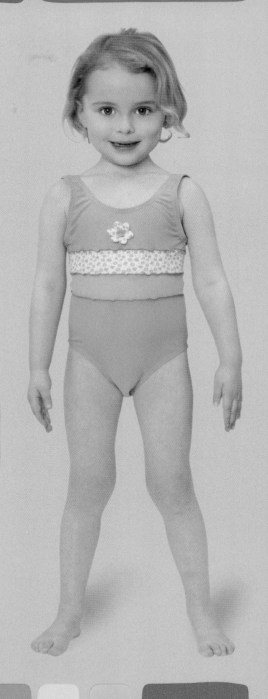

PRAYER FOR TODAY
Tell God how you feel about swimming.
Dear God, I love/am scared of swimming because

....

Amen.

The people in today's story have to swim through a stormy sea. Read Acts 27:21–26, 33–38, 43–44.

Pocket money

Each week, Milly puts some of her pocket money in her piggy bank. She is saving up to buy a new doll! But she doesn't put all her pocket money in the bank. She gives some of her money away to boys and girls who do not have as much as she does. When God has given us so much, it is good to share what we have with others.

We may not have lots of money, but Jesus is pleased when we give what we can to help others. See Luke 21:1–4.

PRAYER FOR TODAY
Dear God, thank you for all you give to me. Help me to use my money to help others. Amen.

New Shoes

Zac has some new shoes. He really likes them! They are also very useful. Zac's shoes will keep his feet warm and dry in the cold, wet weather. Shoes come in all sorts of shapes and sizes: ballet shoes, football shoes, snow boots, and slippers. Do you have a favorite pair of shoes?

PRAYER FOR TODAY
Dear God, thank you for my shoes. My favorite shoes are my

....

Amen.

What kind of shoes are we told to put on as Christians? Read Ephesians 6:13–17.

"I'm sorry!"

What happens when you argue or fight with your brother or sister? Do your mom and dad sort things out or send you to your room? Or do you say "I'm sorry" quickly and make friends again? Jesus tells us that saying "I'm sorry" and forgiving each other is the best way. It's hard to do, but Jesus will help us.

PRAYER FOR TODAY
Sometimes we get upset and fight, we know it's not good, we know it's not right.
Help us to say we're sorry, help us to love, just like you, our Father above.
Amen.

Today's story in Genesis 50:15–21 is about Joseph's brothers saying they were sorry for being mean to him.

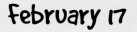
Best friends

Do you have a special friend who you love to play with? Trent's best friend is Olivia, and Olivia's best friend is Trent! They play together and share their toys. Do you know that Jesus wants to be your best friend? He wants to be with you always. He even wants to share his home in heaven with you!

PRAYER FOR TODAY

Dear Jesus, it's amazing that you want to be my friend. I want to be friends with you, too.
Amen.

Find out about Jesus' home in heaven and how to get there. See John 14:1–6.

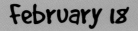

My feet

God has given us ten toes for wiggling and two feet – perfect for tickling! What a good thing God gave us feet! If we didn't have feet we wouldn't be able to stand up, walk, or hop. Feet work very hard, so we have to treat them well. If we don't, they start to smell! How do you look after your feet?

PRAYER FOR TODAY
I'm glad you gave me feet, God! If I didn't have feet I wouldn't be able to

....
Amen.

Today's story is about a man whose legs and feet don't work properly. Read Mark 2:1–12.

All different!

Some people are small, others are tall. Some people are fat, others are thin. God made us all different shapes and sizes. Look in a mirror with your friend and you will see that your eyes, your nose, and your ears are different. Even your hands are different shapes and sizes! God made you very well. He likes what he has made!

PRAYER FOR TODAY
Dear God, thank you for making us the way we are. Thank you for loving each one of us so much. Amen.

Psalm 139:1–6, 13–16 tell us how wonderfully God has made each one of us. Amen.

Day and night

God made the day and he made the night. Can you think of some differences between daytime and nighttime? God made bright light for the day so that plants and trees would grow and so that we could see to eat, work, and play. He made it dark at night so we would rest and sleep.

PRAYER FOR TODAY
Dear God, you made the day and the sun so bright, you made the moon and dark, dark night, you made the year, the day, the hour, you made it all with your great power! Amen.

Find out what God thought about making light. Read Genesis 1:3–5.

Special times

Schooltime, dinnertime, story time, bath time. Can you think of some more times in the day? We have special times for eating and times for playing, resting, and sleeping, too. What's your favorite time of day?

PRAYER FOR TODAY
Dear God, thank you for all the different things I do every day. My favorite time of day is

....
Amen.

God has a special time for everything. See Ecclesiastes 3:1–8.

A safe place

Do you have a special place at home where you feel snug and safe? Sophie loves her big armchair. She snuggles here when she wants to watch television or when she gets tired. I'm very glad God has given me a safe and cosy home.

PRAYER FOR TODAY
Dear God, thank you for my home. My favorite place, where I feel safe, is

....

Amen.

Being God's friend is like being in a safe place. See Psalm 18:2.

A frightening program

Sophie sits in the big chair to watch television. She likes watching television but sometimes the programs get a bit scary. What do you do when that happens? Do you turn the television off, watch something else, hide behind a cushion, or sit on your mom's or dad's lap?

PRAYER FOR TODAY
Dear God, I know you keep me safe from harm. So when the TV makes me scared, help me to turn it off! Amen.

God wants us to watch TV programs that will help us, not ones that will make us scared. Read Philippians 4:8.

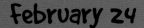

In today's story, music makes a king feel much better. Read 1 Samuel 16:14–23.

A favorite song

I'm glad that God gives people the skill to play instruments and make music. Music can make us feel happy. It can make us want to clap and dance. A special song can help us feel better when we are sad or frightened. What music do you like best? Do you have a favorite song?

PRAYER FOR TODAY
Dear God, I love music, especially

....

Thank you for the people who compose the music and play it. Amen.

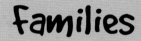

families

Who is in your family? Do you have a photo of you, your mom and dad, your grandparents, and all your aunts and uncles? We smile for photos, but we don't always smile with our families. God knows that we get angry with each other. He wants us to love each other by saying we're sorry and forgiving each other.

PRAYER FOR TODAY
Thank you for my family, God. Please help us to say we're sorry to each other and to forgive each other, too. Amen.

Joseph makes friends with his brothers even though they have been cruel to him. Read Genesis 45:1–14.

Shouts of praise!

What a big shout! I expect you can shout like that, too! Can you think of places where you are allowed to shout and places where you have to be quiet? We can be as loud as we want when we thank God – in fact the Bible tells us to shout our praises to show God how much we love him!

PRAYER FOR TODAY
I love to clap,
I love to shout,
GOD'S THE BEST,
without a doubt!
Amen.

Psalm 100 says the whole world should shout how great God is!

feeling excited

How do you feel the day before your birthday, or the morning that you are going somewhere special? I know some children who are going to Disneyland. They are very excited! What do you do when you are excited? Do you dance around and jump up and down, clap your hands and shout? Or do you smile a lot and have "butterflies" in your tummy?

PRAYER FOR TODAY
Tell God about something really exciting.
God, I get really excited when

....
Amen.

Read 2 Samuel 6:12–15 and find out why King David is so excited.

Taking turns

Everyone wants to have a turn on the slide! But there's only room for one at a time. What would happen if one child pushed in and got on the slide or the swing first? I think it would make the others angry and sad, don't you? The children don't want to make each other sad, so they are all waiting patiently for their turn.

PRAYER FOR TODAY
Dear God, it's hard to wait when I want to go first. Help me learn to take turns. Amen.

Jesus tells a story about people who always want to be first. Find it in Luke 14:7–11.

Helping others

Anna likes the slide, but her little brother gets frightened when he is at the top. Can you guess how Anna helps him? Sometimes she lets him sit in front of her and they go down together. Sometimes she talks to him, telling him how brave he is and how much fun it is sliding down. Can you remember someone helping you?

PRAYER FOR TODAY
Thank God for the person who helps you. Thank you, God, for

....

Show me how I can help others, too. Amen.

God helps us so that we can help others. See 2 Corinthians 1:3–4.

Tiny animals

How many small creatures can you think of? God made each of them and he cares for every one. Isn't that amazing? He wants us to help him care for all the little animals he has made. How could you do that?

PRAYER FOR TODAY
Decide what you could do to help and then tell God.
Dear God, I want to help you look after

....

I'm going to

....

Amen.

Jesus talks about a tiny creature in today's reading. Can you guess what it is? Read Luke 12:6 to find out.

Watering flowers

God wants us to care for the flowers, plants, and trees he has made. Olivia is busy looking after her sunflower. What would happen if she forgot to water it? What else does Olivia need to do to make sure her sunflower grows?

PRAYER FOR TODAY
Dear God,
show me what I need to do
to care for what you've made,
I've got my watering can and
shovel, my garden fork and spade!
Amen.

Read Genesis 1:9–13 to find out how God first made the plants and flowers.

Annoyed and angry

Oh dear! Milly and her friend Jen are annoyed with each other! Does that ever happen to you and your friends? When we are in a bad mood or angry we might want to do things that we know are wrong. But that only makes things worse! If you feel angry, talk to God. He knows how you feel and he wants to help you.

PRAYER FOR TODAY
Dear God, it makes me feel better knowing you care and that you want to help me even when I'm in a bad mood! Amen.

Read what Psalm 37:8 says about being angry.

A bad mood

What do you do when your friend is in a bad mood? Perhaps you leave her alone for a while, or try to get her to play again. But you don't need to stop being friends with her. God is like that with us. He never stops being friends with us no matter how cross or grumpy we are.

PRAYER FOR TODAY
You love me whether I'm grumpy or glad, angry or sad. Thank you, God, for being the best friend ever! Amen.

When your friend is in a bad mood, the words in Ephesians 4:2–3 will help you.

Water

Imagine a world with no water! We wouldn't be able to make tea or coffee. We wouldn't be able to wash our dishes, our clothes, or ourselves. We would get dirty and quickly fall ill. God makes sure we have clean water because he knows how much we need it. So the next time you have a drink, don't forget to thank him!

PRAYER FOR TODAY
For water to drink and keep us clean, thank you God! Amen.

Even when they were in the desert, God made sure his people had water to drink. Read Exodus 17:3–7.

Help with Clothes

Oh-oh! Josh is stuck. He needs help to take his T-shirt off. Getting dressed and undressed can be tricky. What do you find difficult to put on or take off? Who helps you? Remember to thank God for all the people at home and at school who help you with your buttons, buckles, and zippers!

PRAYER FOR TODAY
Dear God, some clothes are difficult to put on and take off. Thank you for

....,

who helps me. Amen.

We all need people to help us. Even Paul asked his friends to help him with his clothes. Read about it in 2 Timothy 4:13.

Shopping

Who do you go shopping with? Do you know that God is with you when you are at the stores? He knows when we get bored waiting for mom and dad to pay. And when we can't make up our minds which toy to choose! God is interested in everything we do.

PRAYER FOR TODAY
Tell God what you do and don't like about shopping. Dear God, I like shopping

because.....................,

but I don't like......................
Amen.

God is interested in everything we do because he made us and he loves us. Read Psalm 139:1–3.

A baby brother

At first Josh was pleased that God had given him a new brother. But when baby Harry came home from hospital, Josh got crabby, because mom was always busy with Harry. It is great to have a new sister or brother, but sharing mom and dad with someone else can be hard. God knows how you feel. You can talk to him, and he always listens.

Today's story is about a big sister who takes care of her baby brother. Read Exodus 2:1–10.

PRAYER FOR TODAY
Talk to God about someone you know who has a new brother or sister.
Dear God, help my friend

....

to love his new brother/sister. Amen.

Rise and shine!

Wake up! Get out of bed! God has made a whole new day for us. What shall we do today? Is it a school day or a holiday, a sunny day or a stormy day? Whatever we do today, whether we are happy or sad, God is with us. He loves us all day long.

PRAYER FOR TODAY
Jesus,
when I'm yawning,
in the morning,
"Stay with me, today,"
I pray!
Amen.

God's love is constant, all the day long. Read Psalm 92:1–3.

"Hello, God!"

What a big yawn! Do you yawn and stretch when you wake up? What else do you do? Emily likes to say "hello" to God at the start of the day. Some mornings she talks to him about what she has planned to do. But sometimes she just says, "What shall we do today, Jesus?"

PRAYER FOR TODAY
Jesus, it's great that I can talk to you any time of the day. Thank you for listening to me. Amen.

King David talks to God in the morning. Read Psalm 5:3.

Building a fort

Alice and Len have had fun making a fort under the table. On rainy days, they make a fort inside and when it is nice, they make a fort out in the garden. They love making forts together. Isn't it great that God gives us friends to play with? Who makes forts with you?

PRAYER FOR TODAY
Forts are great fun, God!
Thank you for my friend

....

We have fun together.
Amen.

Paul likes making tents. In Acts 18:1–3 he finds some new friends, who also make tents. What are their names?

Safe and cozy

I like forts, don't you? I feel safe and cozy in my fort. Sometimes I pretend it's a house, or a cave, or a tent. I fill my fort with my favorite things. I can hide there all alone or have a picnic inside with my friends. What do you like doing in your fort?

PRAYER FOR TODAY
I make my fort under a chair,
in a cardboard box or
anywhere!
Thank you, God, for places
to play,
and people to play with
every day!
Amen.

Forts can also be a good place to take refuge and hide. Where did David hide when he was escaping from King Saul? Read 1 Samuel 24.

Feeling guilty

Emily has been naughty. She knows she has done something wrong and feels uncomfortable inside. She is feeling guilty. Have you ever felt like that when you have done something wrong? I have! When we feel guilty, it is God's way of telling us we are wrong and that we need to say "I'm sorry" and put things right.

PRAYER FOR TODAY
Dear God, when I know I have been naughty, please help me to say "I'm sorry."
Amen.

In today's story, Jonah feels guilty because he knows he has disobeyed God. See Jonah 1:1–4,7,11–12.

"I'm sorry"

You and I can be naughty, like Emily. Sometimes we disobey our moms and dads. We hurt our brothers, sisters, and friends by what we say and do. We can be rude and selfish. God wants us to love him and each other, and when we don't it makes him sad. So when we have been naughty, we must say we're sorry to God.

PRAYER FOR TODAY

Dear God, I'm sorry for all the things I do that make you sad. Help me to love you and to love others, too. Amen.

Find out who makes God very sad in today's story. Read Genesis 6:5–8.

Loving our brother or sister

It's great to have a brother or sister! But we don't always feel like loving them, do we? Sometimes we make each other angry. And then we say and do things that aren't loving at all. Jesus wants us to love each other even when we are crabby. It's hard, but he can help us not to shout or be rude or mean. Just ask him!

PRAYER FOR TODAY
Dear Lord Jesus, I need your help to be kind and loving when my brother/sister makes me angry. Amen.

When Martha gets upset with her sister, she tells Jesus how she feels. See Luke 10:38–42.

Cleaning

I wonder if you help your mom and dad. There are lots of ways we can help them. Can you think of some? Chloe helps with sweeping. She is very good with the dustpan and brush. She makes sure she gets all the dirt in the dustpan! How do you help at home?

PRAYER FOR TODAY
Jesus,
I can clean, I can sweep,
I can put my toys away,
I can dust and polish, too,
helping Mommy every day.
Amen.

Find out why the person in today's story sweeps the whole house! Read Luke 15:8–10.

Good Friends

What do you like about having friends? Jen likes playing with Milly – they play all kinds of make-believe games. Milly loves showing Jen all her favorite toys and treasures. They love talking, are always laughing, and have great fun together!

PRAYER FOR TODAY

Thank you, Lord Jesus, for my friend

....

I like my friend because

....

Amen.

Paul always thanks God for his special friends. See Philippians 1:3–8.

friends care

Friends show they care in hundreds of ways. When Milly is feeling sad, Jen tries to cheer her up. When Jen falls down, Milly rushes to help. Milly and Jen listen to each other, help each other, and stand up for each other. How do you show your friends that you care?

PRAYER FOR TODAY
Thank you, God, for friends who share, friends who love, and friends who care. Help me to be a good friend, too, to love and care, just like you. Amen.

David has some good friends. How do they show that they care? Find out in 2 Samuel 17:27–29.

Cleaning Up

Do you ever make a fuss when your mom or dad asks you to do something? Milly's mom has asked her to put her toys away. Milly hates cleaning up. Sometimes she makes a fuss, but today she is doing a good job. Milly's mom will be really pleased. And so will God! He is glad when we obey our moms and dads cheerfully.

PRAYER FOR TODAY
Dear God, there are some things I don't like doing! Help me to do them cheerfully. Amen.

When your mom or dad asks you to do something, remember what the Bible says! Read Colossians 3:20, 23.

Going to school

Katie likes going to school. She walks with her friend, Chloe. How do you get to school? Do you walk or do you go by car or bus? Next time you are going somewhere, remember to thank God. Thank him for your car, or for the bus, or thank him that you can walk.

PRAYER FOR TODAY
Thank you for the bus and thank you for the train. Thank you for the car that keeps me dry when it rains. Thank you for my feet that take me everywhere. Thank you, God, for all these things that show how much you care. Amen.

In today's story, Jesus sends his friends out on a long walk. See Luke 10:1–9.

A windy day

God makes the wind. He makes the gentle breeze that cools your face and the howling gale that can blow down a tree. You can't see the wind, but you can see what the wind does and you can feel it. How do you know if it is a windy day?

PRAYER FOR TODAY
Thank you for the wind that cools the hottest summer day and brings the clouds to give us rain then blows them all away again! Amen.

In today's story, God sends a strong wind to help Moses and the Israelites. Read Exodus 14:10–22.

feeling excited

Alice is going to be a fairy in her nursery school concert. She is very excited. When Alice is excited, she talks a lot! I'm glad God gives us exciting things to enjoy. What do you get very excited about? How do you show you are excited?

PRAYER FOR TODAY

Lord Jesus, sometimes I'm quietly excited, like a secret safe inside, but now I'm loudly excited as the feeling just won't hide! Amen.

How do people show they are excited when Jesus comes to Jerusalem? See Matthew 21:1–11.

Sad or mad

Olivia is sad and Trent is mad. Can you guess why? Have you ever been left out? How did you feel? Whether we are unhappy, angry, fed up, or lonely, God cares. He is our best friend. We can talk to him at any time. He always understands.

PRAYER FOR TODAY
Sometimes I get angry,
sometimes I get sad,
but knowing that you care
for me, dear God,
that makes me glad.
Amen.

David talks to God about how he feels. Read his prayer in Psalm 55:16,17,22.

Sharing

George is keeping all the sweets to himself. He looks happy but he's made his friends sad. What do you think he should do? It isn't always easy to share, but God can help us. God has shared all he made with us so he can help us share our things with others.

PRAYER FOR TODAY
Thank you, God, for sharing your world with me. When I find it hard to share, please help me. Amen.

Read John 6:1–13. It's all about a boy who shares his picnic.

Special jobs

What do you want to be when you grow up? There are so many different jobs we can do. Do you do any jobs at home already? Think of something you can do this week to help your family. God may have a special job for you to do!

PRAYER FOR TODAY
Dear God, I want to do a job today. Show me what to do. Thank you for people who work hard for me, like

....

Amen.

The people in today's reading are asked to deliver a letter. Find out more in Acts 15:22–23.

Mr. + Mrs. P Faulkner
33 Braid Rd
Morningside

Sam Barber
124 Station Road
Lewisham London
SE13 PQR

Rachel Potts
Pond Hondia
Place Looe
Cornwall PL13 1LF

Mick and Betty Oxley
Box 279
Route I
Cressent City
Florida
32012
USA

I want it!

When we really want to have something, we might try to grab it or take it without asking. Daniel knows he mustn't do that but he wants the vacuum cleaner so much that it has made him very sad. When we are upset because we can't have what we want, we can talk to God. He understands and will help us.

PRAYER FOR TODAY
Dear Lord Jesus, thank you for my toys. Help me not to snatch or take toys away from others.
Amen.

God has given us good rules about how to live happily together. See Exodus 20:15–17.

Clothes

Think of all the different clothes you have. There are clothes for summer and clothes for winter, clothes for parties and clothes for getting messy. There are clothes with stripes, checks, spots, patterns, and sparkly bits. They come in all sorts of colors, with pockets, hoods, buttons, Velcro, and zippers. What do you like to wear?

PRAYER FOR TODAY
Thank you for my clothes, God.
I like wearing

....

the best.
Amen.

In today's story, Joseph's dad gives him something special to wear. Find out what it is in Genesis 37:3–4.

Brothers and sisters

This is Katie and her brother, Andrew. Some brothers and sisters look like each other and some look totally different. Do you look like anyone in your family? I look like my brother but God made us different in lots of ways. Everyone in your family will be different, too. You are all special to God.

PRAYER FOR TODAY
Dear God, it is great to know I'm special to you. Thanks for making me the way I am.
Amen.

Today's story is about twin brothers. They are very different. Read Genesis 25:21–28.

Caring for the lambs

Farmers who take care of sheep are called shepherds. In the springtime, shepherds work very hard taking care of the sheep and their newborn lambs. If a sheep gets out of the field, the shepherd goes to find it. He brings it safely back. Jesus said that God is like a shepherd because he cares for us and wants us to be safe with him.

PRAYER FOR TODAY
I'm really glad you love me, God. Thank you for taking care of me all the time. Amen.

You can find Jesus' story about the shepherd in Luke 15:3–7.

A ship at sea

Look at my ship! It can sail the stormy seas! Sometimes the waves are huge, the ship rocks, and I hold on tight. When we are in trouble, we can call to God. He always listens.

PRAYER FOR TODAY
If I'm happy, sad, or in trouble,
you're always with me,
God. Thank you.
Amen.

Read Acts 27:27–44 and find out how God rescues Paul from a shipwreck.

favorite foods

Isn't it great that God has given us so many different things to eat? As we get bigger we try new foods and flavors and decide if we like them. When I was little, I didn't like spicy food, but now I love it. What did you like eating when you were a baby? What's your favorite food now?

PRAYER FOR TODAY
Dear God, thank you for making food with different tastes and flavors. I like

....

the best! Amen.

Read Matthew 3:1–6 to find out what John the Baptist eats.

A hungry tummy

Our bodies need food to keep working. When your body needs more food, it lets you know – your tummy starts rumbling and you feel hungry. God made us and he knows we get hungry and need food. He made the plants and animals so that we would have plenty to eat. Isn't God good?

PRAYER FOR TODAY
Tummy's rumbling,
I am hungry,
Lord God, please give me food to eat!
Amen.

What food does God give his people when they are hungry in the desert? Find out in Exodus 16:1–3, 11–15,31.

April 2

Drawing

If you want to draw well, you have to keep on trying. Don't give up, and if it doesn't go well, try again! We often have to practice hard to get things right. God can help us to keep going and not to give up.

PRAYER FOR TODAY
Dear God, I find

....

difficult to do. Help me to keep on trying and not to give up. Amen.

The Bible encourages us not to give up following Jesus. See Hebrews 12:1–3.

Getting ready

Zac is excited. It's his birthday soon. He is looking forward to his birthday party. Can you think of all the things Zac and his mom have to get ready for the party? Jesus has invited you and me to the party in God's kingdom. We don't know when it will be, but it will be a great party!

PRAYER FOR TODAY
Dear Jesus, thank you for inviting me to your party. Please help me get ready. Amen.

Who is ready for the party in Jesus' story? Read Luke 14:15–24.

Good Friday

Good Friday is a special day when we think about Jesus. Children don't go to school and stores are sometimes closed. It's a sad day because we remember how Jesus died on a cross. Some people go to church on Good Friday, others think quietly about what happened, or talk to God about it. What could you do to remember Jesus today?

PRAYER FOR TODAY
Dear God, help me to think about Jesus today.
Amen.

The Bible tells us what happened to Jesus on Good Friday. Read about it in John 19:16–18 and 28–30.

Waiting for Easter

Do you like Easter eggs? You can decorate real eggs, or eat chocolate ones. Can you wait until Easter comes before you eat them? Jesus' friends had to wait three days before he was alive again. But that made it even more exciting when Easter Sunday finally arrived!

PRAYER FOR TODAY
Dear God, I find it hard to wait for things to happen. Help me to be more patient.
Amen.

Find out more about what happened on Good Friday in John 19:38–42.

Jesus is alive!

Easter Sunday is a very happy day because Jesus comes back to life again! On Good Friday, his body is placed in a tomb and a large rock is rolled across the door. But when Jesus' friends come on Easter Sunday, they find the stone has been rolled away. Jesus isn't there – he's alive! Isn't that amazing?

PRAYER FOR TODAY
Dear God, it's amazing that you made Jesus alive again.
Thank you!
Amen.

Read the story of Easter in Matthew 28:1–7.

Chocolate egg!

Look at my egg! I love looking at it. But if the shell breaks, we'll find something even better inside! Easter eggs can remind us of the Easter story. Jesus died on the cross on Good Friday, but God brought Jesus back to life! That's a bit like finding the special new life inside a real egg. Jesus died so that we can all be friends with God!

PRAYER FOR TODAY
Dear God, thank you that
I can be your friend.
Amen.

Find out how pleased Jesus' friends are to see him again in Matthew 28:8–10.

Lonely

Daisy is feeling lonely. No one wants to play with her. Daisy is feeling sad because no one wants to be her friend. If you ever feel like Daisy, just remember that God always wants to be your friend. He never leaves you on your own. Even though you can't see him, he is there. He loves you.

PRAYER FOR TODAY

When no one wants to be with me,
when no one seems to care,
I know that you're my friend, dear God,
you love me and you're always there.
Amen.

No one wants to be friends with Zacchaeus. Find out what happens when he meets Jesus in Luke 19:1–10.

A rainbow

Look what I've just made! We've been learning more about God and how much he loves us all. It's lots of fun to meet together at church. We sing songs and listen to stories. I love it!

PRAYER FOR TODAY
Dear God, help me to learn more and more about you.
Amen.

Read Acts 2:44–47 and find out what the first Christians do.

Lots of languages

Isn't God amazing? He has made us all so different. We look different and sound different. We even speak to him in different languages. Some of these friends are saying "hello" in their own language. Can you work out who speaks French, who can speak Russian, who speaks Chinese, and who speaks English?

PRAYER FOR TODAY
Dear God, it's amazing that we can talk to you in so many different ways. It's wonderful that you understand us and love us all. Thank you. Amen.

我很好。

Bonjour

Whatever language we speak, God wants us to praise him. Read Psalm 148:11–13.

Different foods

Molly's grandma lives in China and eats rice for breakfast. Sophie's grandma lives in France and has croissants for breakfast. Jen's grandma lives in Antigua and has mango for breakfast. What do you have for your breakfast? We live in different countries and eat very different food from each other, but God cares for us all wherever we are.

Hello

¡Hola!

Zdravstvuite

PRAYER FOR TODAY
China, America, France, Nepal, thank you, God, for loving us all. From north to south and east to west, our Lord God, you are the best!
Amen.

When Daniel has to go to a distant country, God is with him. See Daniel 1.

Exciting stories

What kind of stories do you like? Do you like exciting adventures or picture stories? Jesus told all kinds of stories. He wanted people to know how much God loved them. Crowds of people sat down and listened to Jesus. Sometimes they stayed all day! He must have been a great storyteller!

PRAYER FOR TODAY
Dear God, thank you for stories that help me learn something new. Amen.

Read one of Jesus' stories. See Matthew 13:1–9.

Learning to listen

It's story time. Where do you listen to stories? Perhaps you have stories at school, at church, or at the library. These children are sitting still and listening very carefully. It's not easy to be quiet and still. When you find it hard to listen, ask Jesus. He will help you.

PRAYER FOR TODAY
Jesus, when I find it hard
to sit still and listen,
please help me.
Amen.

Jesus' friends listened very carefully to Jesus' story about two builders. Read Matthew 7:24–27.

Being happy

What makes you happy? Do you love dressing up, like Trent? Maybe going to the park makes you happy or playing with your best friend. Being Jesus' friend is best of all. The Bible says that when we are God's friends and stay close to him, we'll be really happy.

PRAYER FOR TODAY
Why not thank God for the things that make you smile.
Dear God, thank you for

....

It makes me really happy.
Amen.

**Jesus' friends were very sad when he died. Find out what makes them happy again.
See John 20:19–20.**

Walking the dog

George's dad asked George to take the dog for a walk. George didn't really want to because he was watching elevision. But he did what his dad asked. George's dad was really pleased. I think God was pleased with George, too, because God wants us to obey our dads. What sort of things does your dad ask you to do?

PRAYER FOR TODAY
Dear God, sometimes I don't do what my dad tells me. I'm sorry. Please help me to obey him. Amen.

God is our "dad" in heaven. Read Ephesians 6:1 to find out what he wants you to do.

Hands

Think of all the things you do with your hands. You use them to hold a fork, lift a bag, build a tower, or throw a ball. You use them to pet a dog, stroke a cat, blow a kiss, and wave "hello." But when you pinch, shove, and hit, you are using your hands to hurt others. God wants our hands to help not to hurt.

PRAYER FOR TODAY
Jesus, you gave me hands to help and love, please help me not to pinch and shove. Amen.

Jesus uses his hands to help and love. Find out how he helps in today's story. See Mark 1:40–42.

Being Friendly

We know that pinching or kicking is unfriendly. But we are also unfriendly when we tease people, will not let them join our game, and refuse to talk to them. Jesus wants us to be friendly and kind to everyone. If you see someone being teased or left out, what could you do to be friendly to them?

PRAYER FOR TODAY
Dear Jesus, I know I've sometimes been unfriendly. I'm sorry. Help me to speak kindly and invite others to play with me.
Amen.

Find out who is friendly to Paul when he is left out. Read Acts 9:26–28.

Grandparents

This is Megan with her grandma. We all have grandmas and grandads. They are the moms and dads of our moms and dads. What do you call your grandparents? Do you have special names for them? It doesn't matter whether they live just around the corner or far away, our grandmas and grandads love us and care for us.

PRAYER FOR TODAY
Add the names of your grandparents to the prayer and tell God why you love them.
Thank you, God, for

...................and....................

I love them because................
Amen.

Naomi is very happy when her grandchild is born. See Ruth 4:13–16.

close up . . . and far away!

Try looking at something that is very close. What happens to your eyes? Now think of the farthest thing that you can see. God designed eyes specially to see close up and far away. Isn't that amazing? God is so clever!

PRAYER FOR TODAY
Thank you, God, for my wonderful eyes that see tiny ants and stars in the skies! Amen.

Psalm 139:14 tells us how cleverly and carefully God made us.

Beautiful flowers

God created all the plants and trees. He thought up huge leaves, round leaves, tiny leaves, and spiky leaves. The reds and yellows, pinks and blues of all the flowers were his idea. He made sure there were plants for us to eat and plants for the animals, birds, and insects to eat. What a wonderful world God has made!

PRAYER FOR TODAY
God, I look at the trees,
I look at the flowers,
I see your great love,
I see your great power.
Amen.

Find out what God thought about the plants and trees he created. See Genesis 1:11–13.

Useful plants

God has given us so much to enjoy. Think of all the beautiful and useful plants and trees he made. Did you know that we make French fries, chocolate, and orange juice from plants and trees? Perfumes and medicines come from plants, too. God must love us a lot to give us all these good things!

PRAYER FOR TODAY
Dear God, you've made a beautiful world with so many good things. Thank you for giving us so much. Amen.

Psalm 104:1,14–17 is a "thank you" song to God for making a world full of good things.

friends

I love playing with my friends. Isn't it great that God has given us so many friends to play with? Today Daniel has chosen to play with Chloe and Amy, but yesterday he played with Zac and Josh. Who do you like playing with? Do you choose different friends to play different games?

PRAYER FOR TODAY
Thank you, God, for all my friends,
we laugh and talk and play,
we love to run and build and
paint, having fun all the day.
Amen.

Find out how many special friends Jesus chooses in today's story. See Mark 3:13–19.

God's Friend

God wants us to be his friends. Isn't that amazing? He thinks we are really special. He loves us so much that he sent Jesus to make sure that we could be his friends forever. Nothing beats being God's friend!

PRAYER FOR TODAY
Dear God, it's awesome that you want me to be your friend. Thank you for choosing me. Amen.

God wants his friends to be like him. Colossians 3:12–14 explains how we can do this.

caring for animals

God told us to take care of his animals. If you had a pet rabbit, dog, or hamster, how would you keep it safe from danger? Did you know that leaving trash on the ground can be dangerous for wild animals and birds? When we put our cans and plastic wrappers in a trash can, we are helping to keep God's wild animals safe, too.

PRAYER FOR TODAY
Dear Lord God, I want to take care of your animals. Show me how I can keep them safe. Amen.

Jesus talks about himself as the Good Shepherd who cares for his sheep. Read John 10:11–16.

Cuts and bruises

Frankie was running really fast, then – trip – she fell down. Her knees started bleeding. The teacher cleaned them and put on bandages. Frankie's knees feel really sore today. But do you know what's amazing? In a week or so they will nearly have healed! God has given us bodies that can do amazing things, like healing when they get hurt.

PRAYER FOR TODAY
Ouch! It really hurt when I fell!
Dear God, please make me well.
Amen.

Jesus made lots of people well again. See Luke 4:40.

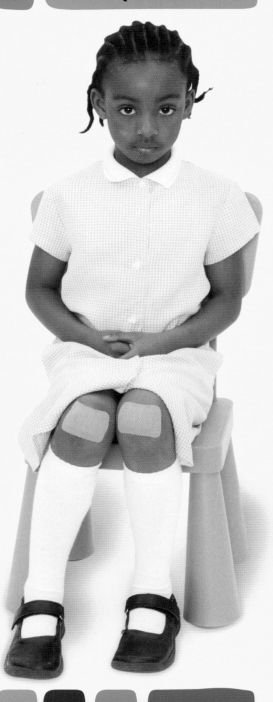

Counting

It's fun learning to count. Try counting the blocks Emma and Toby are using! How many green blocks can you see? Take a look around you! God has given us a world full of things to count. Let's get counting!

PRAYER FOR TODAY
Counting's fun, God, one, two, three,
four, five, six, just watch me!
seven and eight and nine and ten,
watch me count them all again!
Amen.

Look out for all the numbers in today's story! See Luke 9:12–17.

A clever brain

When we count blocks or build a tower, we have to think hard. We concentrate so that we don't lose count or make the tower fall. We also use our brain when we concentrate on painting a picture or when we listen carefully to a story. God has given us a clever brain and he is pleased when we think hard and listen carefully.

PRAYER FOR TODAY
Dear God, help me to listen carefully to you and think hard about what you want me to do every day.
Amen.

The two women in today's story are both busy. Which one is busy listening to Jesus? Read Luke 10:38–42.

Big Cats

Did you know that the lion belongs to the cat family? In fact, it is one of the biggest cats God made. God made all sorts of cats: some with spots and some with stripes. He made the cheetah the fastest animal of all. And he gave the snow leopard long, white, woolly fur – can you guess where it lives?

PRAYER FOR TODAY
Dear God, thank you for making so many different, wonderful animals.
Amen.

Read Genesis 2:18–20 to find out how the animals get their names.

Fierce or friendly?

Lions look so cuddly, but I know they are very dangerous. God made them fierce and strong with powerful legs and sharp teeth so that they could catch their food. God cares about all the creatures he has made – the cuddly ones and the scary ones. We all belong to him.

PRAYER FOR TODAY
When I'm frightened of

....,
please help me, God.
Help me to remember that
you made the
........................, too.
Amen.

Who did God rescue from a hungry lion? Find out in Daniel 6.

Mealtime

We're all sitting down together.
We're going to share a meal.
Dad's worked hard to cook us our
favorite food. Max put the plates
on the table. I got upset with Max
because I wanted to do that job.
But Dad said, "No shouting at
the table!" I took a deep breath.
I'm going to try and be nice
to my brother!

PRAYER FOR TODAY
Dear God, thank you for
mealtimes together. Help us to
be kind to each other.
Amen.

**Read Ephesians 4:31–32 to
see how God likes us to
behave with each other.**

Where does food come from?

Dad cooked the meal, but where did the food come from? From the supermarket, of course! But before that? From the farm or factory! But before that? From God! God is incredible – he has made so many things that we can eat and enjoy. What's your favorite food?

PRAYER FOR TODAY
Tomatoes, beans, spaghetti, or meat – Thank you, God, for the food we eat! Amen.

Read about a wonderful picnic in Luke 9:16 and see how Jesus thanks God for food.

My legs

I'm very glad God gave us legs!
There are so many things we need
our legs for – walking, running,
hopping, jumping, cycling,
swimming, and dancing. Try using
your legs now! Can you balance on
one leg? Can you hop like a frog?
Can you point your leg and toes,
like Emily? How about sitting
cross-legged? Amazing you!

PRAYER FOR TODAY
I'm standing on one leg, God,
now watch me hop!
Look at me, I'm running,
my legs never stop!
Amen.

**Find out who is walking and
who is dancing in today's story!
See Exodus 15:19–20.**

New skills

We have to learn to use the body that God has given us. When we were babies we learned to crawl and walk. Now that we are older we learn to do things like swimming, playing football, and dancing. Emily is learning ballet. It was tricky at first but now she loves it! Are you learning to do something new?

PRAYER FOR TODAY
Dear God, I'm learning to

....
Help me to keep going even when it gets difficult.
Amen.

**We can use our bodies to thank God, too.
Find out what King David does in 2 Samuel 6:14.**

A new skirt

Aisha is really pleased! Her neighbor is good at sewing and has made her a new skirt. People who make clothes work hard. They have to measure, cut, pin, and sew! And it's difficult to make things fit exactly, because everybody is a different size and shape. God made us all different. That's what makes you really special!

PRAYER FOR TODAY
Dear God, thank you for my clothes and for the people who made them. Amen.

Look at 1 Samuel 2:18–19 and find out what Samuel's mom makes for him to wear.

Small animals

God made lots of small animals. Can you think of some? Zac's hamster is small but very fast. When he starts to run it tickles Zac and makes him laugh. The hamster runs everywhere. I think Zac will have to pick him up before he runs away. Remember to be gentle with him, Zac!

PRAYER FOR TODAY
I like the small creatures you made, God. My favorite is

....

Amen.

God wants us to take care of his little creatures.
See Genesis 1:28

Guilty

Quite often we know we have done something wrong even before our moms and dads scold us. We know we have done wrong because we feel bad inside. We feel guilty. When we feel guilty, God wants us to say we're sorry and make things right again. He always forgives us. He will help us put things right again.

PRAYER FOR TODAY
Lord God, when I know I have done something wrong, help me to say "I'm sorry" and make things right.
Amen.

Psalm 51 is a song about saying "I'm sorry."

obeying our moms and dads

It's not much fun being scolded! We get scolded when we don't do what our moms or dads tell us. And we are in trouble when we do something they told us not to do! When you find it hard to obey, talk to God about it. He wants to help us to obey our moms and dads.

PRAYER FOR TODAY
I've been scolded again, God! That makes
..................................……….
times today! I need your help right now, dear God, to listen and obey. Amen.

Jesus learned to listen to his mom and dad. See Luke 2:51.

Weddings

What makes a wedding such a special occasion? We wear our best clothes, we throw confetti, and we have a party. But did you know that it is promises that make a wedding special? The bride and groom make wonderful and important promises. They promise God and each other that they will love and care for each other for the rest of their lives.

PRAYER FOR TODAY
Pray for the people you know who are married.
Dear God, please help
....
to keep the promises they made on their wedding day.
Amen.

The bride and groom promise to love each other. Read
1 Corinthians 13:4–8, which explains what love is like.

Parties

I love parties, don't you? Jesus went to parties, too. Have you ever been to a wedding party? They are a bit like birthday parties. The families and friends of the bride and groom celebrate the important occasion with delicious food and drink, a special cake, presents, music and dancing, and lots of fun.

PRAYER FOR TODAY
Parties are fun, God, parties are great! I love to dance and laugh, and eat lots and lots of cake! Amen.

In today's story, Jesus goes to a wedding party with his family and friends. Read John 2:1–11.

Twins

Jack and Louis are twins. They may look the same but they are different in lots of ways. Jack likes playing with trains, but Louis prefers building with bricks. Jack's favorite color is blue, but Louis' favorite color is red. Each one of us is different and each one of us is very special to God.

PRAYER FOR TODAY
It's great you made us different, God, and I'm glad you made me ME! Amen.

Today's story is about twins who are very different. Read Genesis 25:19–28.

Doing what you're told

Do you do what your mom asks you? I wonder if you are like Josh. Sometimes he does what mom asks right away, but other times he doesn't do what mom asks at all! He doesn't mind helping with the vacuuming, but he hates picking up his toys! But God wants Josh to listen to his mom and do what she says. He wants you to do that, too!

PRAYER FOR TODAY

Dear God, sometimes I find it hard to do what my mom says. Will you help me? Amen.

Do you know what makes God happy? Find out in Colossians 3:20.

Fighting

We all argue and fight sometimes, even with our friends. Can you think of things you argue or fight about? Maybe you and your friend sometimes fight over toys, or argue about whose turn it is, or even argue about who is the best! Jesus knows we argue and fight, that's why he tells us to love each other, to say "I'm sorry," and forgive each other.

PRAYER FOR TODAY
Jesus, when I start to argue and fight with my friends, help me to stop and say "I'm sorry".
Amen.

In today's story, Jesus' friends are arguing. See Luke 22:24–27.

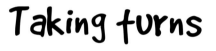

Taking turns

What would you do if you and your friend both wanted to play with the same toy? I bet you would take turns. And I bet you would let your friend have the first turn, because that's what friends do! And that's just what Jesus would want you to do, too!

PRAYER FOR TODAY
Jesus, I don't always want to let my friend go first. Please help me. Amen.

Read Matthew 7:12 to find out how Jesus wants us to treat other people.

I won't say "I'm sorry!"

Can you guess what is wrong with Molly? She hit her sister and called her names. Molly knows it was wrong but she doesn't want to say she's sorry. Have you ever felt like that? God wants us to say "I'm sorry" to each other. It can be a really hard thing to do, but if we ask God, he will help us.

PRAYER FOR TODAY
Dear God, sometimes I am like Molly. Please help me to say "I'm sorry" when I have done naughty things. Amen.

Jesus tells a story about someone who says "I'm sorry."
Read it in Luke 15:11–21.

My best friend

When no one wants to be my friend and no one wants to play with me, it makes me feel sad, angry and lonely all at the same time. When other friends don't want to be with me, Jesus always does. He is the best friend of all. He promises to be our friend for ever. And he always keeps his promises!

PRAYER FOR TODAY
Thank you, Jesus, for being my friend. When I feel sad and all alone, help me remember you are with me always. Amen.

Jesus makes friends with people no one else wants to be with. See Luke 19:1–10.

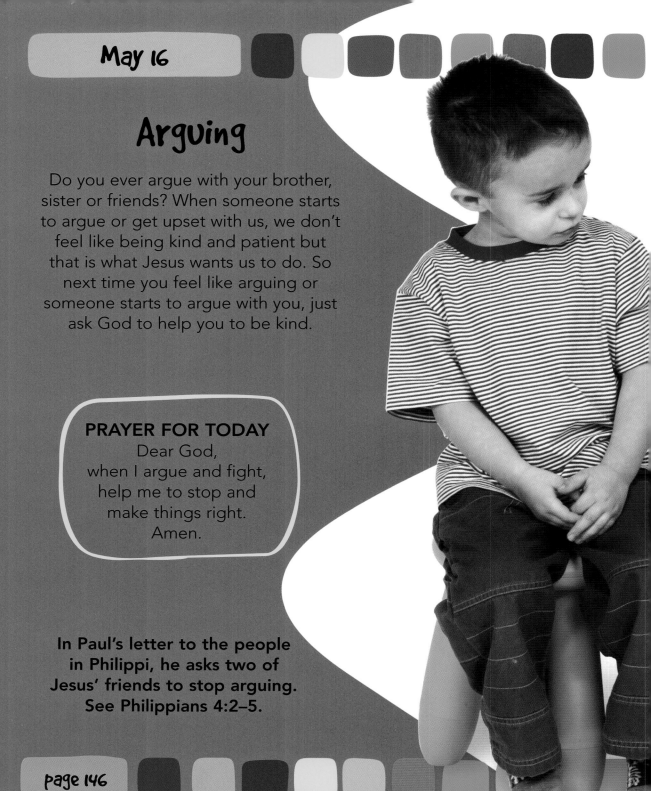

Arguing

Do you ever argue with your brother, sister or friends? When someone starts to argue or get upset with us, we don't feel like being kind and patient but that is what Jesus wants us to do. So next time you feel like arguing or someone starts to argue with you, just ask God to help you to be kind.

PRAYER FOR TODAY
Dear God,
when I argue and fight,
help me to stop and
make things right.
Amen.

In Paul's letter to the people in Philippi, he asks two of Jesus' friends to stop arguing. See Philippians 4:2–5.

Saying "I'm sorry"

Sophie and Toby have been quarreling. Both children need to say "I'm sorry" to each other. Even though Sophie started the argument, she doesn't want to say "I'm sorry" first. Do you ever feel like that? Toby is doing what Jesus would want. He is saying "I'm sorry" first, so that he and Sophie can be friends again.

PRAYER FOR TODAY
Dear Jesus, when I find it hard to say "I'm sorry," please help me. Amen.

Jesus tells a story about a man who says "I'm sorry" to God. He becomes friends with God again. Read Luke 18:9–14.

Going to the doctor's

Breathe in, breathe out! Can you remember going to the doctor's? What was it like? Sometimes we might not want to go, but doctors are very good at finding out what's wrong with us. When we're sick, God provides special people to help us.

PRAYER FOR TODAY

Dear God, thank you for doctors and nurses.
Amen.

Read Mark
1:30 and
find out who
Jesus helps.

Someone to hold you

If you get sick, who usually takes you to the doctor? Megan is glad that her mom is with her. She feels safe sitting on her mom's knee and knows that her mom will hold her tightly if something hurts. God is with us, too, when things hurt. He holds us in his hands.

PRAYER FOR TODAY
Dear God, thank you that you are always with me, even at the doctor's or the hospital.
Amen.

In today's story, sick people are brought to Jesus. Read Mark 1:32–34.

caring for plants

God has filled his world with all kinds of plants. He wants us to take care of them. Can you think how you could do that? We can grow plants from seeds, or help to water a houseplant, or weed a garden. And when we are out in the countryside, we can enjoy wild flowers by looking at them instead of picking them.

PRAYER FOR TODAY
Creator God, thank you for making so many different flowers and plants. I want to help you by looking after them.
Amen.

Find out what God thinks about the trees, plants, and flowers he has made. Read Genesis 1:11–13.

Farmers

Farmers work very hard to grow food for us to eat. They plant all kinds of trees, bushes, and plants. They care for them until the crop has grown. Some plants take too long to pick by hand, so the farmers use special machines. How do you think a farmer would harvest oranges? What about potatoes? What about wheat?

PRAYER FOR TODAY
Dear God, take care of the farmers as they plant, sow, tend, and grow food for us all to eat. Amen.

In Matthew 13:1–9, Jesus tells a story about a farmer.

Pets

We keep all sorts of animals as pets – dogs, cats, rabbits, birds, fish, and even lizards! God wants us to love and care for them. We show that we love them when we talk to them, stroke them, and pet them. We show that we care when we feed them, give them exercise, and clean their homes.

PRAYER FOR TODAY
They squawk and scratch, hiss and bark, crawl, hop, and run, we thank you, God, for all our pets, we love them, every one! Amen.

Find out how the poo[r] man cares for his pet i[n] today's story. See 2 Samuel 12:1–3.

Setting the table

God wants us to help each other. We can help our friends, we can help our brothers and sisters, and we can even help our moms and dads. Can you see how Max is helping his mom? There are lots of other ways we can help at home. Can you think of some?

Find out what Peter and John do to help Jesus. Read Luke 22:7–13.

PRAYER FOR TODAY

Tell God how you help your mom and dad. Dear God, I help my mom and dad when I

....

Amen.

Taking medicine

Joel isn't feeling well, but he's being brave about taking his medicine. Did you know that a lot of medicine comes from plants? God cares about us so much, he created plants that can help us get better quickly. Scientists figure out which plants help us and use these plants to make different medicines. Isn't that clever?

PRAYER FOR TODAY

Dear God, thank you for medicine that makes us well again. Amen.

The man in today's story is ill. He has to do something very strange to get better. Read 2 Kings 5:1,9–14.

All alone

Have you ever been lost in a big, busy place? It's very scary when we can't find mom or dad. We feel very lost and alone. When you think you are lost, talk to God. He looks after us wherever we go. He will help you and keep you safe.

PRAYER FOR TODAY
Dear God, when I'm lost and scared and all alone, please hold me close and bring me safely home.
Amen.

Psalm 91 tells us to trust God because he can keep us safe.

Home

I love my home. It's where I live. It's the place where I feel safe. But the best thing about home is living with people I love and who love me, too! Who lives in your home? God is so good to give us homes and people to love. We must remember to thank him.

PRAYER FOR TODAY

For my warm, cozy home,
where I'm never on my own,
for the people who love me,
my very special family,
thank you, Lord God.
Amen.

The young man in this story is very glad to be home again. See Luke 15:11–24.

Amazing stories

Sophie loves sitting on her mom's lap and listening to her tell a story. Who tells you stories? Do you have a favorite story? There are stories about princesses, heroes, magic rings, and talking animals. But Sophie's favorite story is not a made-up one. It is true. It really happened. It is the story of Jesus!

PRAYER FOR TODAY
Jesus, I love stories.
My favorite is

....
Amen.

Read a part of the amazing story of Jesus in Luke 24:1–12.

Fun in the sun

Olivia and George think life is "cool!" They have been swimming, playing games, eating ice cream, and having great fun together in the sun. Can you count all the good things God has given you? Start by thinking of all the people you love, then think of the games you like to play, and the places you like to go.

PRAYER FOR TODAY
Wow, God, you're great! You've given me so many good things. THANK YOU FOR THEM ALL!
Amen.

Psalm 149:1–3 is a song telling God how great he is.

Show mom you love her!

How does your mom show you that she loves you? Does she cook food for you, read you stories, clean your clothes, give you hugs and kisses, take you to special places, tuck you into bed at night, and take care of you when you are hurt or ill? How do you show your mom that you love her?

PRAYER FOR TODAY
Thank you for my mom, God. Help me to show her that I love her today, tomorrow, the next day, and always! Amen.

Jesus didn't want his mother to be alone after is death, so he asked his riend John to look after er. Read John 19:25–27.

Wonderful flowers

God made all the flowers beautifully. He gave them each their own special shape, color, and smell. He made flowers that are good at climbing up walls, flowers that keep close to the ground, and flowers that stand up tall like soldiers. If God cares about each one of these flowers, we can be sure he cares for us, too.

PRAYER FOR TODAY
Dear God, it's wonderful that you care about the tiniest flower. And even though I'm little, I know you care for me, too. Amen.

Jesus told us that God cares about all the little things. Read Luke 12:27–28.

Sun and rain

God makes sure that there is enough sun and rain for plants to grow. He makes sure there is enough food for animals and birds to eat. God keeps the world going. He never stops caring for it. He asks us to care for it, too.

PRAYER FOR TODAY
Dear God, it's awesome how you keep the world going. I'm glad you're in charge. Amen.

Psalm 147:7–9 is a Bible song that talks about how God looks after his world.

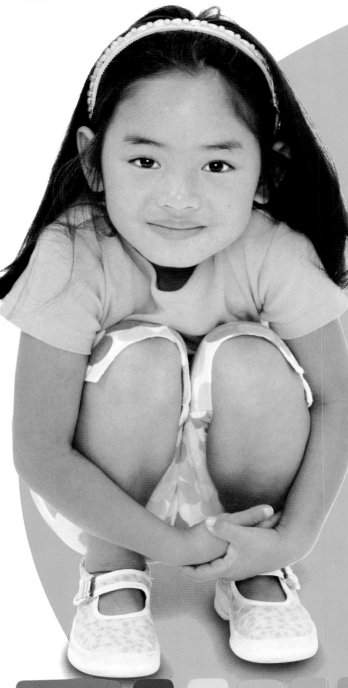

My body

God has given us wonderful bodies. Let's see what yours can do! Can you crouch down on the ground? Can you twirl round and round? Can you stretch up really high? Can you blink or close one eye? Can you hop or jump or clap? If you can, thank God for that!

PRAYER FOR TODAY
Thank you, dear God, for my body and for all the amazing things I can do with it! Amen.

Psalm 139:13–14 tells us that God created every part of us.

Scared of the dark

Sophie is scared of the dark. So she keeps a flashlight right next to her bed and she leaves her bedroom door open to let in some light. And whenever she feels really scared she talks to God. Talking to God helps her to remember that God will take care of her all through the night.

PRAYER FOR TODAY
Loving God, I know you take care of me through the night. Whenever I am frightened, please hold me tight. Amen.

When you feel scared going to bed, read Psalm 4:8.

Walking together

Katie and Chloe love walking to school together. They skip, run and talk nonstop! Jesus and his friends liked walking together and talking about God. Jesus would tell his friends stories about the way God wanted them to live. It was fun being with Jesus. And though you can't see him, Jesus is with you, too, even as you go to school.

PRAYER FOR TODAY
Jesus, I want to walk with you,
Jesus, I want to talk with you,
Jesus, I want to be with you,
the whole day through.
Amen.

In today's story, Jesus and his friends are walking together, talking about something really important. Read Mark 9:30–32.

Starting school

Katie was a little scared when she started school. Her friend Chloe, who is older than she is, promised she would walk to school with Katie and look after her in the playground. Chloe is a really good friend – she has kept her promise. When we keep our promises, we are like God. He always keeps his promises.

PRAYER FOR TODAY

Dear God, you always keep your promises. Help me to keep mine, too. Amen.

King David makes a promise to his friend. Find out how he keeps his promise in 2 Samuel 9:1–10.

Naughty Katie!

Oh-oh! I think Katie has been naughty. What happens when you do something you have been told not to do? Do your mom and dad scold you? God has given our moms and dads the job of teaching us to be kind. God wants us to listen to them.

PRAYER FOR TODAY
Lord God, I'm sorry for not doing what mom and dad tell me. Help me to obey them. Amen.

In today's story, Jesus listens to his mother. Read Luke 2:51–52.

How to behave!

I don't like being scolded, do you? I know a good way of making sure you never get into trouble. Would you like to know the secret? Love your mom and dad, speak to them kindly, and do what they ask you. When you do that, everyone is happier and God is really pleased!

PRAYER FOR TODAY
Dear God, I'm sorry for being rude and disobedient. Help me to love my mom and dad and do what they ask me.
Amen.

Ephesians 6:1–3 is a message from God especially for you.

A watery home

Do you like wearing goggles? I love swimming under the water, but I can't hold my breath for long! But God made lots of amazing creatures that live under the water all the time. It's their home. How many sea creatures can you think of?

PRAYER FOR TODAY
Dear God, thank you that you give everyone a home, even the fish! Amen.

Read how God made the sea creatures in Genesis 1:20–23.

colorful sea creatures

Some fish have spots, like my swimsuit! But others have stripes, or multicolored scales. Lobsters have shells, and jellyfish have . . . jelly! God has made so many colorful creatures. Maybe one day you can visit an aquarium and count how many different kinds you can see.

PRAYER FOR TODAY
Spots, stripes, and shimmering tails,
Thank you for fish, lobsters, and whales!
Amen.

Read the amazing story of how a large water creature helps a man! See Jonah 1:17.

Tall George!

I wonder how tall George will be when he is older? Do you think he will be as tall as his big brother? George and Charlie don't know now how tall they will be when they are grown-up or whether they will live to be 100 years old. But God does. God knows all about George and Charlie, and you and me!

PRAYER FOR TODAY
Dear God, it's fun getting bigger and growing older. I'm going to be

....

on my next birthday!
Amen.

God is amazing. He knows about all the days of our life. See Psalm 139:15–16.

Being ill

Toby is feeling tired and achy. One minute he's hot, then he starts to shiver. I think he's ill, don't you? When you are ill, do your mom and dad tuck you into bed, take your temperature, and give you medicine? God cares for us when we are ill, too. We can ask him to help us get better quickly.

PRAYER FOR TODAY
Ask God to help someone you know who isn't feeling well. Loving God, please help

....

get better soon.
Amen.

Today's story is about someone who is ill and tucked into bed. See Mark 1:29–31.

Giving away a toy

Look at all these toys! The children have been sorting out their toys at home. They have each chosen something special to bring to church to give as a present. All the toys will go to children who don't have many things to play with. God gives us so much to enjoy. It's great to be able to give to others, isn't it?

PRAYER FOR TODAY
Dear God, help me to share my special things with other people. Amen.

Read Acts 2:44–45 and find out about people who love God and share all that they have.

Exciting days

Sophie has just heard she is going to be a flower girl in a wedding. How exciting! We don't all get to be flower girls, but God gives us lots of other exciting times. Can you think of some of the exciting days you have had? What did you do? Where did you go?

PRAYER FOR TODAY
Tell God about your most exciting day.
Dear God, thank you for the day I

....

It was great!
Amen.

The children in today's story are excited because someone very special has come to town! Read Matthew 21:14–16.

A big mouth

Try singing loudly with your mouth closed! Now open your mouth and sing! Which is easier? Now try singing "la, la, la" in front of a mirror. What happens to your tongue? Mine goes up and down! God gave us tongues, lips, and mouths so we can sing songs to him. Choose your favorite song and sing it to God now!

PRAYER FOR TODAY
Dear God, with my voice, lips, and tongue, I'll sing you a "thank you" song.
Amen.

David loves singing. Find out what David sings about in Psalm 34:1–8.

A mouth for eating

We use our mouth to sing and talk, but what else do we use it for? Eating, of course! God has given us teeth to cut and chew our food, and a tongue to taste different flavors. I love the taste of strawberries. What's your favorite flavor?

PRAYER FOR TODAY
God, you are great!
You made all of me.
Thank you for my
mouth, my teeth,
and my tongue.
Amen.

What do the people eat in today's story? Read Mark 6:35–44.

Planting a tree

It's great that God made so many different plants and trees. If you want to grow your own tree, you need a seed. If you plant an apple seed and give it water and light, very slowly it will grow and grow and GROW. It takes years for trees to grow, so you will have to be very patient!

PRAYER FOR TODAY
Thank you, God, for the trees so tall, it's awesome they start as seeds so small!
Amen.

What seed does the man plant in Jesus' story? Find out in Mark 4:30–32.

Together!

It's fun playing with our friends! But have you noticed that when you do a jigsaw puzzle with your friends, you finish it faster? It's the same when it's time to clean up. When everyone helps and we all work together, we soon get the job done.

PRAYER FOR TODAY
Together we talk and straighten up,
together we work and play.
Together we live to love you,
God, help us love one another today.
Amen.

Paul is glad to have lots of friends to work with. How many are in today's reading? See Colossians 4:7–14.

Yummy food!

God has given us all sorts of food: sweet and sour, plain and spicy, crunchy and chewy, food for forks and food for fingers! What's your favorite? I love roast potatoes, peaches, chocolate, milkshakes, and ……. In fact, God has given us so many delicious things to eat, it's hard to choose!

PRAYER FOR TODAY
Dear God,
Thank you for all the delicious food you give us to eat
Amen.

Jesus feeds lots of people. Find out what he gives them in Matthew 14:15–21.

I can't wait!

It's hard to wait, isn't it? Olivia and George have to wait for their friend, Trent, before they can eat the treats. God wants Olivia and George to learn to wait patiently (and that means waiting quietly without making a fuss). When do you have to wait?

PRAYER FOR TODAY
Dear God, I find it hard waiting for

....

Please help me to wait patiently. Amen.

Today's story is about a man who waits for a very long time. See Luke 2:25–33.

Tiny animals

If you lift up a stone in the park or look carefully at a plant, you might find some of the tiny creatures God has made: centipedes, scurrying ants, shiny black beetles, and bright red ladybugs. Do you know that a centipede has 100 legs? It's great fun discovering the amazing creatures God has put in his wonderful world!

PRAYER FOR TODAY

Lord God, thank you for making shiny beetles, squirmy worms, and slimy slugs.
Amen.

God made all the creatures in the world: the huge and the tiny. See Genesis 1:24–25.

Dreams

I wonder what Sophie is dreaming about? Sometimes she has good dreams that make her smile or laugh in her sleep. But sometimes her dreams make her wake up feeling frightened. When that happens, her mom comes to comfort her. They sing a song. Then they talk to God and ask God to give Sophie sweet dreams.

PRAYER FOR TODAY
I'm lying quietly in my bed,
the busy day still in my head.
Dear Jesus, help
me sleep and rest,
and dream the dreams
I like the best!
Amen.

When Pharaoh has a strange dream, Joseph helps him. Find out how in Genesis 41:1–40.

Sing a song

Singing is great fun! You can dance and sway to the beat, stand very still, or clap your hands in time. It doesn't matter if you forget the words – just hum along. Singing can make you feel really happy. Sing your favorite song now! God loves to listen.

PRAYER FOR TODAY
I want to sing and dance,
I want to praise you, God!
Amen.

There are some wonderful songs in the Bible. Read Psalm 8:2 to see who can sing to God!

Sing together!

We're singing together! It's easy, but we have to listen to each other, or we would be singing different songs at the same time! That would be a real mess, wouldn't it? People who love God often sing together. They sing about the wonderful things God has done, and how he loves us all.
Do you want to join in?

PRAYER FOR TODAY
Dear God, we sing to you, thank you for the wonderful things you do!
Amen.

In Psalm 100, the whole earth praises God! Can you imagine the sound?

Getting help

What do you do if your friend gets hurt? How do you help her and make her feel better? When Olivia fell and hurt her knee, Joel asked a grown-up to help her. Can you remember a time when you hurt yourself? Who helped you?

PRAYER FOR TODAY
Dear God, thank you for

....
who helped me when I was hurt. Please help me to be a caring friend, too.
Amen.

The man in today's story cannot walk. Find out how his friends help him. Read Mark 2:1–12.

Caring for others

I wonder if you've ever scraped your knee, bumped your head, or been stung by an insect. When we get hurt at home or at school, we need someone to look after us, to give us a hug, wash our wounds, put a bandage on the scrape, ice on the bump, and cream on the sting.

PRAYER FOR TODAY
Thank you, God, for bandages,
for tissues, creams and rubs,
for people who look after me,
with loving care and hugs.
Amen.

Jesus tells a story about a man who is hurt. Find out how he gets better in Luke 10:30–35.

The slow tortoise

The tortoise moves v-e-r-y s-l-o-w-l-y. God likes the tortoise, just the way it is. God made some creatures that walk slowly, some that slither, others that trot. Can you think of their names? God made one animal that runs faster than all the others. Do you know what it is called?

PRAYER FOR TODAY
Fast or slow, big or small,
Dear Lord God, you made them all!
Amen.

Discover which bird runs really fast. Read Job 39:13–18.

favorite toys

God has given us a wonderful world to live in.
We have great toys and games to play with.
What is your favorite? Trent loves playing outside
on his bouncy ball. Bouncing is such fun!

PRAYER FOR TODAY
Sometimes, Jesus, I wear myself
out, I ride, I hide, I climb and shout.
I like to bounce, I love to run,
I hop, I skip, it's loads of fun!
Amen.

**The Bible reminds
us to thank God
for all he gives us.
See Psalm
104:33–34.**

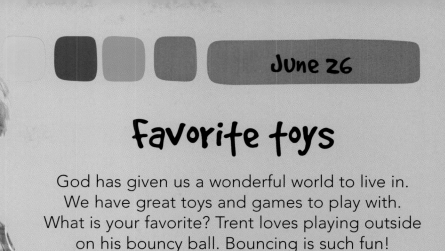

Eyes to see!

Our eyes help us every day. What would happen if the children tried to catch the bubbles with their eyes shut? I think they would bump into each other, don't you? Try walking, eating, or putting on your shoes with your eyes closed! Be careful! Isn't it great that God gave us eyes to see?

PRAYER FOR TODAY
Dear God, you made me very well. Thank you for giving me eyes to watch, look, and see.
Amen.

The man in today's story cannot see at all.
Read Luke 18:35–43.

friends

When you are hurt or feeling ill, your friends help you and care for you. A friend will hold your hand, pat your arm, or give you a hug or a kiss. A friend will sit quietly with you when you don't want to run around or play. A friend understands when you are sad. Let's thank God for giving us friends!

PRAYER FOR TODAY
Thanks, God, for giving me friends who care for me. Help me to be a caring friend to them, too. Amen.

The caring people in today's story ask Jesus to help their friend. Read Mark 7:32–37.

Squabbling

Playing in the wading pool is such fun! But when I want to put more water in and my friend wants to pour the water out – then there's trouble! We end up fighting and squabbling, instead of playing. If we tell each other what we want to do, listen carefully to each other, and agree how we will play, we have much more fun!

PRAYER FOR TODAY
Dear Jesus, when I'm playing with my friend

....

help me to listen to him/her and think about what he/she wants to do. Amen.

Philippians 2:4 tells us to think about what others want.

Playing with water

Splish! Splash! Splosh! I love playing with water, don't you? Think of all the different places where you play with water: in the bath, at the swimming pool, or outside in a wading pool. You may even have a special place at nursery school for playing with water. I like pouring it from a watering can. What do you like doing with water?

PRAYER FOR TODAY
Thank you, God, for water,
splish, splash, splosh!
It's perfect for paddling
and having a blast!
Amen.

Today's story is about a man waiting to get into a special pool of water. Read John 5:1–9.

Caring for animals

There are lots of ways we can care for God's animals. We can feed the birds or look after pets. At the zoo it is the keeper's job to take care of the animals. This zebra has a kind keeper who works hard cleaning the enclosure and making sure that the zebra has enough grass and hay to eat and clean water to drink.

PRAYER FOR TODAY

Thank you, God, for zoo keepers, farmers, and vets, who take care of your animals. Help me to take care of your world and your animals too. Amen.

Genesis 1:24–26 tells how God made all the animals and gave humans the important job of caring for them.

Let's pretend

God has given us clever minds so that we can imagine. Li and Ying are good at imagining. They love playing "let's pretend" games. They pretend they are heroes, like Superman and Peter Pan. They take it in turns to be the hero and rescue each other. Do you play games like that? Who do you like to be?

PRAYER FOR TODAY
I'm glad I can imagine, God. When I play "let's pretend", I like to be

....
Amen.

There is a real hero in today's story. He isn't big or strong, but he knows God will help him win. Read 1 Samuel 17:32–50.

Helping each other

It's snack time at school. George is helping to pour the drinks. Are you good at pouring? George is concentrating hard so that he doesn't spill any drink. The children take turns to pour the drinks and pass out the snacks. I think God must be pleased with them all. He loves it when we help each other.

The Bible tells a story about a little slave girl who helped her mistress in a very important way. Read about it in 2 Kings 5:1–14.

PRAYER FOR TODAY
Tell God what you do to help someone else.
Dear God, I help

....
Amen.

I'm thirsty

Trent is really thirsty and can't wait for George to stop pouring. He is so thirsty, I think he will drink his juice all in one gulp! I wonder whether Trent will remember to say "thank you?" It was very kind of George to bring Trent a drink, wasn't it? Who brings you drinks when you are thirsty?

PRAYER FOR TODAY
Thank God for the kind people who give you drinks at home or at school. Amen.

Today's story is about a kind person who helps Abraham's servant when he is really thirsty. See Genesis 24:17–20.

Building sand castles

I love the beach. I like digging holes, making sand castles, and burying my feet. One day, I tried to count how many tiny grains of sand there were in my bucket. But there were too many to count. The Bible says that's just like God's family. There are more of us than there are grains of sand on the shore. Isn't that amazing?

PRAYER FOR TODAY
Wow! It's great to be part of your family, God. It's amazing that you love each one of us!
Amen.

Abraham was the father of God's huge family. Read Genesis 22:15–18.

feeling shy

Going to a new place or meeting someone new can make us feel shy. When Alice feels shy, she doesn't want to look or talk, she just wants to hide. She holds on tightly to mom or dad. God wants to help us when we feel like that. Although we can't see him, he is always with us. We are safe with him.

PRAYER FOR TODAY
Dear God, when I feel shy, help me to remember that I'm safe with you. Amen.

If you feel shy, remember what the Bible says. See Proverbs 18:10.

Happy birthday!

It's Milly's birthday! She's six today! Milly loved being five but she is very excited to be six. Birthdays are special days when we thank God that we are one year older. Milly and her mom and dad said a prayer to thank God for Milly's birthday. What else is going to happen on Milly's birthday? Can you guess?

PRAYER FOR TODAY
Dear God, thank you that I am

....
years old. It's fun getting bigger and growing older. Amen.

The Bible tells us about Jesus growing older. Look up Luke 2:40.

A party

What do you like best about birthdays? Milly has presents, a special cake with candles, and party balloons. But she isn't opening her presents or eating her cake. Can you guess why? She is waiting for her friends to arrive for her party. Birthdays are fun with our friends. Isn't it great that God gives us friends to share our special day?

PRAYER FOR TODAY
Dear Lord Jesus, I love having birthdays. I like it when I have my friends

....

with me. Thank you for all of them. Amen.

Find out what happens when Jesus and his friends go to a party. See John 2:1–11.

Sisters

Molly is very glad God gave her a little sister. She loves Alice a lot. And Alice thinks it's great to have a big sister. Do you have a sister? Is she older or younger than you? How do you show her that you love her? Molly and Alice give each other big hugs.

PRAYER FOR TODAY
Thank you, God, for my sister. Help me to love her every day. Amen.

Read about Moses' big sister in Exodus 1:22–2:9

Cuddles

George loves cuddling with his mom. Who gives you a cuddle? George's mom cuddles him when he's sad. She cuddles with him at bedtime and hugs him just to say how much she loves him. George is very glad that God has given him a mom to love him and look after him.

PRAYER FOR TODAY
I like it when I am cuddled. Thank you, God, for my mom. Amen.

Read Mark 7:24–30 and find out how Jesus helps the mom in today's story.

A hurt arm

Chloe fell off the jungle gym. Her arm hurts a lot. It hurts when she tries to move it so she can't put on her shoes or play on the swing. Can you think of other things she can't do while her arm is in a bandage? God knows that Chloe is feeling sad and sore. He knows when you are hurt or feeling ill, too. God always cares for you.

PRAYER FOR TODAY
Jesus, when I'm ill,
you show you care,
when I'm hurt, you're
always there.
Amen.

Read Luke 8:40–56 and see how much Jesus cares for people who are really ill.

A visit to the nurse

God gives us lots of people to take care of us when we are very ill or badly hurt. Chloe's mom and dad took her to see the nurse at the hospital. The nurse bandaged Chloe's arm and made her feel much better. Have you ever had to go to the hospital? Who took care of you?

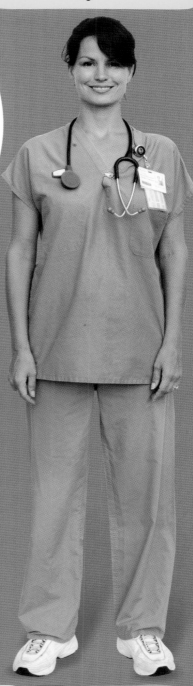

PRAYER FOR TODAY
Thank you, God, for moms and dads, who care for us when we are ill. Thank you, too, for doctors and nurses, who work to make us better. Amen.

Today's story is about a man who cannot walk. Who looks after him? Who makes him well? See Mark 2:1–12.

Playing with friends

Trent likes playing with the construction bricks. Sometimes he plays on his own but he likes it better when his friends play with him. What games do you play on your own? What games are more fun when you have a friend to play with? Every day we can thank God for our friends and our favorite games.

PRAYER FOR TODAY
Thank you for my friends, God. It's great to have friend to play with. I like playing

....

with my friends.
Amen.

God gives us friend and fun because he loves us. Psalm 117 is a song thanking God for his love!

Grabbing

Katie has taken something that belongs to Andrew. Can you see what it is? When someone grabs a toy we are playing with, we feel very sad and cross. God wants us to live happily together, and that's why he says we mustn't take things that belong to someone else. What do you think Katie should do now?

PRAYER FOR TODAY
Dear God, I'm sorry for grabbing and taking without asking. Please help me to play the way you want me to.
Amen.

In Exodus 20:15, God tells his people not to take things from each other without asking.

Ice Cream

Do you know where your favorite food comes from? I love chocolate ice cream. I know that a farmer grows cocoa beans to make chocolate. Another farmer raises cows to make cream. Factory workers mix it all together to make the ice cream. A truck driver brings it to the store and the storekeeper sells it to me! I have to thank a lot of people for my ice cream!

PRAYER FOR TODAY
Thank you, God, for

.... and for

.... ,
who work hard to grow and make it for me.
Amen.

God once provided food and drink for his messenger, Elijah, in a very strange way! What was it? See 1 Kings 17:2–6.

Playing store

Louisa and Rachel love playing store. Do you play store at nursery school with your friends? Rachel wants to be the storekeeper with the cash register. What should Rachel do if she wants a turn? What do you think Louisa should do? Taking turns means Louisa must give up doing something she likes for a little while to make Rachel happy.

PRAYER FOR TODAY
Dear Jesus, sometimes I find it hard to take turns. Help me to think about making my friends happy. Amen.

Whatever we are playing with our friends, we should always be loving. Read 1 Corinthians 16:14.

Trees

Trees are great for climbing and for hiding behind. But they are useful, too! Trees give us wood that can be made into chairs and tables, climbing frames and toys. Do you have any toys made of wood? Paper comes from trees, too! If we didn't have trees, we wouldn't have paper for drawing and painting. I'm very glad God made trees, aren't you?

PRAYER FOR TODAY
Thank you, God, for trees to climb,
for paper, card, and wood,
for all our wooden games and toys.
It's true, God, trees are good!
Amen.

Find out who climbs a tree in today's story! See Luke 19:1–10.

Special clothes

Hope is going to be a flower girl. She has a beautiful dress to wear for the wedding. Weddings are important days. Everybody puts on fancy clothes for the special day. Have you been to a wedding or to another special event wearing your very best clothes? What did you wear?

PRAYER FOR TODAY
Thank you, God, for my special clothes. I remember the day I wore

....
Amen.

Jesus tells a story about a wedding. Read it in Matthew 22:1–14.

fears at night

What do you do when you wake up frightened in the night? Do you run to your mom or dad? Do you hug your teddy really tightly? Do you sing your favorite songs? Whenever you are scared, you can talk to God. He has promised to take care of everyone who turns to him.

PRAYER FOR TODAY
I'm frightened, dear God,
I'm scared, please keep me safe
tonight. Hold me in your loving
arms until the morning light.
Amen.

**If you are scared
in the night,
remember
Psalm 63:6–8.**

Monsters

When it's dark and strange sounds frighten me, I remember that God loves me. When it's dark and shadows make monster shapes on the wall, I remember that God is stronger than any monster. When it's dark and I feel afraid, I talk to God. I know he takes care of me.

PRAYER FOR TODAY
Tell God what frightens you at night.
Dear God, sometimes at night I am scared of

....

Help me remember you are strongest of all.
Amen.

The Bible tells us that God keeps us safe both day and night. Read Psalm 91:4–5.

Let's cook

It's fun playing cooking games! Jim and Melanie are making a pretend cake. They are going to share their cake with their friends. I like making real cakes, too. It's fun to ice and decorate them for my friends. Do you make food for your friends? What do you make?

PRAYER FOR TODAY
Dear God, it's fun to pour and stir,
to bake a cake to share,
and hand it out to all my friends,
to show how much I care.
Amen.

Read John 21:4–14 to find out what Jesus cooks for his friends.

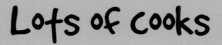

Lots of Cooks

There are lots of people who cook for us. How many can you think of? Mom or dad might cook for us at home, and sometimes grandma or grandpa. Then there are people at school or nursery who make our lunch. How kind of God to make sure there are so many people to cook delicious food for us!

PRAYER FOR TODAY
Dear Lord God, thank you especially for

................................,
who cooks for me. I like it when he/she makes

....
It's my favorite!
Amen.

Today's story is about a very kind woman who cooks some food for Elijah. See 1 Kings 17:8–16.

Books, books, books!

Sophie loves books. She looks at the pictures and then she tries to find the letters she is learning at school. Learning to read can be hard at first, but it won't be long before Sophie can read all the words. Then she will have great fun reading all the wonderful stories about Jesus for herself.

PRAYER FOR TODAY
Dear God, thank you for books and stories. Please help me as I learn my letters and learn to read by myself. Amen.

In today's story, God sends Philip to help a man who is trying to read part of the Bible. See Acts 8:26–31.

Showing love

God wants us to love each other. We show love in lots of ways. We give hugs and kisses, we listen and talk, we help, we share our special things, and we give little presents. Milly saw these beautiful flowers in her garden. She is going to give them to her mom. How do you show your family that you love them?

PRAYER FOR TODAY
Dear God, thank you for my family. Help me to show them that I love them. Amen.

How does the woman in today's story show Jesus that she loves him? Read Mark 14:3–9.

Babies

Have you noticed how noisy and messy babies are? They cry, are sick, and have dirty diapers. But even though they do all those things, they bring us lots of happiness. A baby is a gift from God – a new person to care for and love.

PRAYER FOR TODAY
Talk to God about a new baby that you know. Thank you, loving God, for

....

Help his/her family to take good care of him/her. Amen.

The baby in today's story brings his mom and dad great happiness. Read Genesis 21:1–7.

Let's paint!

Rosa and Amy want to do some painting. Amy can't put on her apron by herself, so Rosa is helping. Isn't that kind? Jesus is pleased when we are kind and help others. I bet you are good at helping, too. What do you do to help other children in your play group or your class at nursery school?

PRAYER FOR TODAY
Thank you, God, for friends that help me. I want to be a helping person, too. Amen.

Read 1 Samuel 20 and find out how Jonathan helps his friend David.

What I do best!

Olivia is good at playing the recorder. Trent plays the xylophone really well. They are each doing what they do best and together they make a good sound! God has made us all different. Some people are good at running, some are good at thinking, and others are good at sharing, helping, or being friendly. What are you good at?

PRAYER FOR TODAY

I'm glad you've made us all different, God. I'm good at

....

and my friend is good at

....

Amen.

In today's story, God uses people who are good at different things to help others. See Acts 6:2–7.

Making music

Do you like making music? Olivia and Trent do! They have been learning to play the recorder and xylophone at school. They have been practicing hard. Now they can play a song about Jesus that they sing at school. But they also like to make up their own songs, to thank God. Can you play an instrument?

PRAYER FOR TODAY
I love to play the triangle, the xylophone and drum, I'll play and sing to thank you, God, for all that you have done!
Amen.

Psalm 150 tells us to praise God with all sorts of instruments. What are they?

Vacations

Did you know that vacations are God's idea? When God finished making the world he gave everyone a vacation. He made a special day each week when we don't have to work or go to school – we can enjoy being with him. We can rest and enjoy everything God has given us. What do you do on your vacation?

PRAYER FOR TODAY
Thank you, God, for vacations. What a great idea! I like to

....

on my vacation.
Amen.

Today's Bible story is about God giving everyone a holiday. Read Genesis 2:1–3.

Excited or worried?

Olivia and Trent are going on a vacation. They are very excited and a little nervous because they don't know what it will be like. Where do you go on vacation? Do you get excited? Or do you sometimes feel worried, too? Whether you go to the mountains, the city, the country, or the seaside, God is always with you.

PRAYER FOR TODAY
Thank you, God, for being with me wherever I go. Please keep me safe when I go to new places.
Amen.

When we are nervous about going somewhere new, we can remember God's words in Joshua 1:9.

Sister love

Do you have a sister? Is she older or younger than you? Emily loves her big sister, Britney. She draws pictures for her at school and gives Britney big hugs. Britney loves Emily, too. She reads to her and plays with her. And when they get cross with each other, they make up quickly. How do you show your sister that you love her?

PRAYER FOR TODAY
Thank you, God, for my sister. Help me to show that I love her even when she makes me mad. Amen.

Jesus said that if we love him we must love our brothers and sisters too! See 1 John 4:21.

feeling grumpy

What do you do when you are feeling grumpy?
When Emily is crabby, she talks to her big sister.
But some days Britney is too busy. God is never too
busy to listen to us. We can tell him how we feel.
And when we remember all the good things God
has given us, we can't feel grumpy for long!

PRAYER FOR TODAY

Think of the many good things God
has given you, and thank him.
Thank you, God, for always listening
to me. Thank you for

.... and

.... Amen.

Read Psalm 13:1 and then verses 5–6 to find out
what makes this sad person cheerful again.

Wet and Wonderful

It roars, it waves, and it crashes. It's salty, wet, and huge! It covers most of the earth. Can you guess what it is? Yes – the sea! It is amazingly deep and full of all kinds of weird and wonderful creatures. And God made it all.

PRAYER FOR TODAY

You make the oceans crash and roar,
you make the swoosh of the
wave on the shore,
you are awesome, you are great,
I thank you, God, for all you make!
Amen.

Today's story is about God making the oceans. See Genesis 1:1–10.

Exploring rock pools

Have you ever wandered around rock pools by the sea? It's amazing to discover all the wonderful plants and creatures God has made. There are all kinds of sea snails wearing all kinds of shells. There are crabs that scuttle sideways and seaweed that smells! What an amazing world God has made!

PRAYER FOR TODAY
God, you made the octopus, seaweed, shrimp, and shell, from oceans deep to rocky shore, you made it all very well! Amen.

Psalm 104 is a song to God, praising him for what he has made. Read Psalm 104:24–25.

Sharing

Jesus wants us to be good at giving and at sharing our toys. Sometimes I do what Jesus says because I want to make others happy. But sometimes I don't want to share at all! I want to keep everything to myself. That's when I need to ask Jesus to help me. When is it hard for you to share your toys?

PRAYER FOR TODAY

I'm sorry, Jesus, for not sharing. I'm sorry for wanting everything myself. Please help me to share my things with others.
Amen.

Find out what Jesus says about giving and sharing. Read Matthew 5:42.

A hot dog

God has given us the important job of loving and caring for his animals. Amber has been running around the garden and now she's very hot. She needs some water to help her cool down. Do you have any pets? How do you take care of them?

PRAYER FOR TODAY
Talk to God about your pet. Dear God, I love my

....

Please help me take good care of it.
Amen.

In today's story, Moses helps to look after someone else's animals. See Exodus 2:16–17.

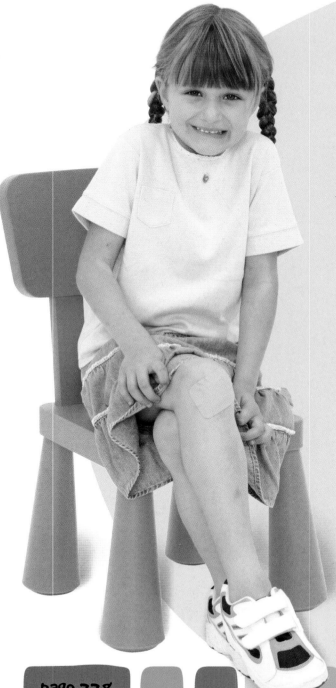

It hurts!

Ouch! Olivia fell off her scooter and scraped her knee. Her mom has washed her knee and put a bandage on. God always sees and knows when we hurt ourselves. He knows how sore Olivia's knee is, so Olivia and her mom have asked God to make her knee get better quickly.

PRAYER FOR TODAY
When I fall,
God's always there.
When it hurts,
God always cares.
Thank you, God,
for loving me.
Amen.

**God loves to make people well.
Read Acts 3:1–10.**

I'm angry!

Do you get mad? I do. Sometimes when we get angry we say or do awful things and that makes God sad. God wants us to talk to him when we're angry. We can tell him exactly how we feel. He always understands. And he can help us to be patient and kind, just like he is.

PRAYER FOR TODAY
Dear God, I'm sorry I do bad things when I'm angry. Please help me to be like you.
Amen.

Find out what God is like in Psalm 86:15.

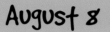

Presents for the bab

All these presents are for Molly's new bab
brother. A new baby is a special gift from
God. Lots of people have sent gifts to sho
how happy they are that he has arrived.
Molly's brother is too little to open them.
Do you think Molly could help him?

PRAYER FOR TODAY
Thank you, loving God,
for new babies. Help us
to look after them.
Amen.

Lots of people are happy
when Jesus is born. Read
Matthew 2:9–12 and find out
what presents he is given.

God's present

I love getting presents, don't you? Did you know that God has given you and me a very special present? It may seem like a strange sort of present, but it is the best present of all. He has given us Jesus to be our very best friend.

PRAYER FOR TODAY
Dear Jesus, I'm really glad you're my best friend. Thank you, God, for giving me such a great present!
Amen.

John 3:16 tells us why God gave us Jesus.

Police

Can you see what Bob is doing? He is pretending to be a police officer. Police officers work very hard night and day to make sure our homes and our towns are safe places to live. They have to be brave and caring to do such an important and dangerous job.

PRAYER FOR TODAY
Dear God, thank you for police officers who work to keep us safe. Please help them and keep them from harm.
Amen.

Nehemiah and his helpers work night and day to protect their city. See Nehemiah 4:1,12–23.

Farmers

Have you ever been to a farm? They can be very noisy places! Think of all the different animals you find on a farm. What noises do they make? The farmer has an important job. He has to take care of God's animals. He makes sure that all the animals have food, clean water, and safe, clean places to live.

PRAYER FOR TODAY
Dear God, who made cows and sheep, pigs and chickens, please help the farmers as they take care of your animals. Amen.

Jacob is good at caring for sheep and goats. You can read about Jacob in Genesis 29–30.

Tiny creatures and huge planets

God controls the whole universe. He planned it all and knows how it all works. He made creatures so tiny you need a magnifying glass to see them. He made planets and stars so far away you can only see them with a telescope. God made it all AND he loves and cares for it. What a great God!

PRAYER FOR TODAY
Wow! You are awesome, Lord God! I'm glad you are in control of the world. Amen.

God knows all about the world he has made. See Job 38:16–41.

Loving our dad

We show our dads that we love them in lots of ways – when we paint them a picture, give them a hug, or do what they tell us to do. God is our "dad," too. He is our Father in heaven. And we can show him that we love him by doing what he says.

PRAYER FOR TODAY
Father in heaven, I love you. Please help me to do what you say.
Amen.

How can we show God that we love him? Find out in 1 John 5:2–3.

Let me shout!

When we feel really excited, we can't keep it inside. We get a bubbly, happy, fizzy feeling that makes us want to jump, run, or dance around. When we are excited, it is hard to keep quiet, isn't it? We can't help shouting or cheering. What do you do when you are excited?

PRAYER FOR TODAY
Hello God,
I get really excited when

....

It makes me want to

....

Amen.

There is a lot of cheering, dancing, and shouting in today's story! Read 2 Samuel 6:12–15.

feeling scared

I wonder what has frightened Matt? What makes you scared? I get scared when I'm high up, on a jungle gym. When I'm frightened, I talk to God. God always listens and he always helps. God often sends other people to help us when we are frightened. And God also helps us to be brave.

PRAYER FOR TODAY
Dear God, I know you care when I am scared. Help me to remember that you can help me and make me brave. Amen.

When David was scared and in danger, God helped him. David wrote this song to thank God. See Psalm 18:1–6.

What is your hair like?

God made us very carefully. We are different shapes and sizes. Even our hair is different. I have long, straight, light brown hair. What about you? What color is your hair? Is it black or brown, red or blonde? Is it thick or thin, straight or curly? Is it long, short, or in-between?

PRAYER FOR TODAY
God made me from my toes to my hair!
You've made everything well, God,
thanks for your care!
Amen.

Judges 13–16 tells the story of the great warrior, Samson. His hair is long to show that he belongs to God.

Every hair on your head!

Do you know how many hairs you have on your head? It would take a very long time to count them all. But Jesus said that God loves you so much and knows you so well that he knows exactly how many hairs you have. Isn't that amazing?

PRAYER FOR TODAY
You're great, God! You know everything about me and you love me. Thank you. Amen.

In today's story, Jesus explains to his friends how much God cares for each of us. See Matthew 10:29–31.

Talking to dad

What's special about your dad? What do you like doing best with him? It can be great fun doing something special. And sometimes it's good just to talk to your dad and tell him about what you've been doing. Jesus said God was our Father. Like our dad, God loves us so much and wants us to talk to him.

PRAYER FOR TODAY
Dear Father God, thank you that you love me so much. Amen.

In Luke 15:11–32, Jesus tells a story about a father and two sons. Find out what happens.

Brush your teeth!

What do you use to brush your teeth? I've got an electric toothbrush. Milly has an ordinary one. I use mint toothpaste. Milly uses strawberry-flavored toothpaste! But we both brush our teeth every evening and every morning. What about you?

PRAYER FOR TODAY
I'm glad you've given me teeth, God. I want to take good care of them. Help me to remember to brush them. Amen.

We need to look after our teeth, because God made them for us. See Psalm 139:13,15.

Crying

I think Jim needs a hug, don't you? We all cry sometimes. We cry when we want someone to know that we are sad or hurt, ill or tired, frightened or lonely. God sees us when we cry and he knows what makes us sad. Even though we can't see him, he is close to us. He wants to comfort us.

PRAYER FOR TODAY
I cry when I am sad,
I cry when I get hurt,
I cry when no one else can see,
but you, dear God, you care for me.
Amen.

God cares about you so much, he knows about every tear. Read Psalm 56:8–11.

feeling sad

Sometimes things happen that make us very, very sad. When someone we love very much goes away or when our pet dies, we can feel sad, angry, and empty inside. Jesus understands how we feel. When sad things happen to you, Jesus will be there to love you and help you. You can talk to him.

PRAYER FOR TODAY
Jesus, I know that you love me. I know that you listen. I want to tell you that I feel very sad about

....
Amen.

In today's story, Jesus is very sad when his friend Lazarus dies. Find out more in John 11:1–3,17,32–35.

Looking after the world

God has made so many different people – men and women, boys and girls. He has put us in different places and different countries. But he has given us all the same important job – to look after his world. There are lots of ways we can do that. Can you think of some?

PRAYER FOR TODAY
O God, you made us all. Help us take care of each other. Help us all to look after your world.
Amen.

It was God's idea to give us the job of looking after his world. Read Genesis 1:26–31.

Caring for each other

The world is full of different people. We look different and we live in different places but God made us all. It was God's idea to make men and women and boys and girls. He wants us to love each other and help each other. When we care for each other, no one is left out or lonely.

PRAYER FOR TODAY
Thank you, God, for everyone,
for friends and family.
Help me, God, to care for them,
the way you care for me.
Amen.

God does not want Adam to be on his own, so he makes a friend for him. Read Genesis 2:18–23 and find out who it is.

Listening to dad

We don't always want to do what our dads tell us. But God has given our dads the important job of helping us grow up. God asks our dads to show us how to make the right choices and how to be good and kind like Jesus. That's why God wants us to listen carefully to our dads.

PRAYER FOR TODAY
Dear God, take care of my dad and help him to teach me about you. Please help me to listen to him. Amen.

Proverbs 13:1 says it is smart and wise to listen to your dad.

Listening to God

God made us, loves us, and cares for us. He is our "dad" in heaven. God loves it when we talk to him. He wants us to listen to him, too. That's why he has given us the Bible so that we can find out what he wants to say to us.

PRAYER FOR TODAY
Dear Father in heaven, I'm glad I can talk to you. Please help me to hear what you are saying to me. Amen.

Jesus came from heaven to show us what our Father God is like. Read John 6:44–47.

August 26

Beach time

Olivia and George have fun in the sun. They are very glad God made the sun because on sunny days they go to the beach. I wonder what they're going to do there? Can you guess? I think they're going to make a huge sandcastle. What do you love doing on sunny days?

PRAYER FOR TODAY
Thank you, God, for
making the sun.
When it's warm and sunny
I have such fun!
Amen.

Today's reading, Psalm 136:1–9, is a "thank you" song to God.

A sunny day

Have you ever heard how much noise the birds make when the sun comes up in the morning? Or maybe you've seen the beautiful colors in the sky when the sun sets in the evening? God has made it all and he wants us to praise him from first thing in the morning until we go to bed.

PRAYER FOR TODAY
I'll thank you in the morning,
I'll praise you all day long,
and in the evening, dear God,
I'll sing a "thank you" song.
Amen.

Psalm 113:3 tells us
to praise God all
day long.

A broken doll

Have you ever broken a friend's toy? Jasmine snatched at Jan's doll and the arm came off in her hand. Jasmine has said "I'm sorry" to Jan, and they are going to see if they can fix it. Saying "I'm sorry" is very important and helps other people to feel better. God likes to hear us say "I'm sorry," too.

PRAYER FOR TODAY
Dear God, I'm sorry for the bad things I have done today.
Amen.

Read 1 John 1:9 and find out how pleased God is when we say "I'm sorry."

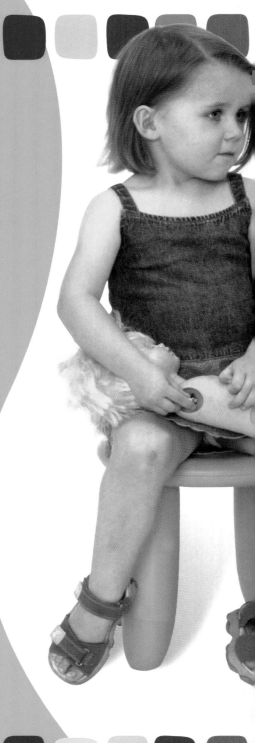

It's OK!

How do you feel when a friend says "I'm sorry" for hurting you or breaking your toy? Jan feels a little better now that Jasmine has said she is sorry, but she still feels a little angry inside. Jan knows that when someone says "I'm sorry," she should try to be kind and forgive them, so that they can be friends again.

PRAYER FOR TODAY
Dear God, help me to forgive other people, like you forgive me. Amen.

The Bible shows us how to be kind. Read Ephesians 4:32.

cats

What a happy cat! Its owner looks after it well. But lots of other people take care of it, too. The vet looks after it when it is ill. The neighbors stroke it and treat it kindly. What animals do you see in the garden or the street? God wants you to be gentle and caring to all the animals that you meet.

PRAYER FOR TODAY
Tell God about the different animals that you see. Dear God, I see

.....................and.....................
Help me to treat them gently.
Amen.

How does God take care of the animals during a big flood? Find out in Genesis 7:1–10.

Waiting patiently

At one o'clock Michael is going to see his grandma. He can't wait! Hurry up, clock! God wants us to learn to wait without making a fuss. That's hard to do! It's hard to wait for food or a drink when we are hungry or thirsty. And very hard to wait when we are excited. When do you find it hard to wait?

PRAYER FOR TODAY
I just can't wait!
I want it now!
It's hard to wait,
God, teach me how!
Amen.

Who is patient in today's story? Read James 5:7–8.

fruit

Just look at those juicy grapes! And that spiky-topped pineapple. Can you count the bananas? Isn't God amazing to make all the different fruits look so tasty? And they smell so good, too. What is your favorite fruit? Eat some today!

PRAYER FOR TODAY
Bananas, peaches, grapes, and plums, thank you, God, for fruit – yum yum! Amen.

Read Numbers 13:23–27 and find out what fruit the people eat.

Sharing

How do you feel if your friend takes the cookie or doughnut that you want? Does it make you feel mad? When we share food, we have to think about what our friends like as well as what we want. It's not always easy, but if we ask God to help us, we will get better at sharing.

PRAYER FOR TODAY
Dear God, help me to share the good things you give me. Amen.

Read 1 Samuel 25:2–20,23–27 and find out what Abigail shares.

All you need

I wonder what Katie has in her backpack. Can you guess? What do you take to school? I bet your mom or dad makes sure you have everything you need for the day. That's just like God. He makes sure we have everything we need – food, clothes, families, friends, love, and so much more! Isn't God great?

PRAYER FOR TODAY
Thank you, God, for being so kind and giving me everything that I need. Amen.

Jesus says we don't have to worry about the things we need because God is looking after us. Read Matthew 6:31–33.

feeling scared

Katie likes going to school now. But on her first day she was very scared. Have you ever been scared going somewhere new? When we are afraid we can talk to God. He is always close to us. And he can help us because God is bigger and more powerful than everything, even the things we are scared of!

PRAYER FOR TODAY

Dear God, when I'm scared, help me remember that you love me and that you will help me.
Amen.

Make up a tune for the words from Psalm 56:3 so you can remember them when you are scared.

Knitting

Have you ever tried to knit? Aisha wanted to learn. But the wool got all tangled up! Her mom is really good – she knits sweaters and socks for the whole family. God has made some people really good with their hands.

> **PRAYER FOR TODAY**
> Dear God, thank you for all the people who make my clothes.
> Amen.

Read Acts 9:36–42 and find the name of a woman who is very kind to others, making all sorts of clothes for them.

Try it again!

If something is difficult, what do you do? Give up, or keep on trying? If you keep on trying, you'll feel so good when you manage to do it! If you are struggling with something, ask God to help you. He always listens!

PRAYER FOR TODAY
Dear God, I find it really difficult to

....
Please help me to keep on trying.
Amen.

Huram is very good at making things. Find out more in 2 Chronicles 2:13–14.

People to care for us

God makes sure there are lots of people to take care of us. There are people to take care of us at home. And there are people who look after us at nursery or school. Who takes care of you at home? It might be mom and dad or grandma and grandpa. You might even have a stepmother or stepfather too. Who takes care of you at school?

PRAYER FOR TODAY
Thank you, God, for all the people who take care of me. I want to thank you especially for

....
Amen.

Joseph isn't Jesus' father but he takes very good care of him. Read Matthew 1:18–25.

Packing up

Hurry up, Aisha! Hurry up, Max! The toys have to be packed away soon. It's moving day tomorrow! Max and Aisha are excited about their new house and they are a little nervous about making new friends. But they know that God is always with them, no matter where they live.

PRAYER FOR TODAY
It's great to know that wherever I go and wherever I live, you are always with me. Thank you, God. Amen.

Nowhere is too far away from God's love. See Psalm 139:7–10.

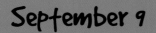
Sharing

This trailer is Zac's favorite toy. It can be hard to share our favorite things – often we don't want anyone else to play with them. Zac is being very kind, sharing his trailer with Anna. God wants you and me to be kind like that. What's your favorite toy? Are you good at sharing it with your friends?

PRAYER FOR TODAY
Dear God, sometimes I'm not good at letting others play with my toys. I'm sorry. Please help me to share. Amen.

The woman in today's story shares something very precious. What is it? Find out in Matthew 26:7–13.

Arguing

"It's mine! Give it to me! I want it!" Sometimes we fight over our toys. God doesn't want us to annoy our brothers and sisters or fight with them. He wants us to love each other. That means that we must learn to share our precious things. And we must learn to treat other people's toys well.

PRAYER FOR TODAY
Sorry, God, I fought and argued with

....
I know you want me to love him/her. Please help me! Amen.

Joseph doesn't get along with his brothers. You can find his story in Genesis 37:2–11.

Happy birthday!

When is your birthday? How old will you be? On your birthday, your mom and dad remember the day you were born. They give you a present to make you feel special. Perhaps they also thank God for giving them such a beautiful, precious child. Yes – that's you!

PRAYER FOR TODAY
Dear God, thank you for loving me. Thank you for my family that loves me, too.
Amen.

Read 1 Samuel 2:18–19 and find out what Samuel's mother gives him as a special present.

Parties

Do you like birthday parties? Isn't it great to have fun with friends? Make sure you don't leave anyone out! God gives us friends to share our special days with. Who will you invite to your next birthday? Ask God to help you make everyone feel really welcome.

PRAYER FOR TODAY
Balloons and cake for everyone,
thank you, God, for birthday fun!
Amen

Jesus eats with people who are often left out. Read Mark 2:15–17.

Reading together

Emily thinks her big sister is great! They play all sorts of games together but Emily's favorite time is when her sister reads to her. Do you have a big sister or brother? What do you like to do together? Isn't God good to give us brothers and sisters to play with?

PRAYER FOR TODAY
Thank you, God, for my brother/sister.
I like it when we

....

Amen.

The brothers in today's Bible story are busy. What are they doing? Read Matthew 4:18–22 to find out.

Bedtime story

What do you do before you go to bed? Maybe you like to have a story time, just like Emily. Did you know that the Bible is a book of God's stories? There are exciting ones and scary ones, sad ones and happy ones. When we read God's stories, we discover what God wants to say to us.

PRAYER FOR TODAY
Thank you for giving us your special book of stories, God. Help me to listen to you.
Amen.

Find out what God says to Samuel when he is tucked into bed! Read 1 Samuel 3.

Fighting Fires

Who would you call if your school were on fire? Firefighters, of course! They are trained to put out fires. They go into dangerous places to rescue people. They work hard to make sure we are safe. I am very glad God has made such brave people.

PRAYER FOR TODAY
Dear God, thank you for our brave firefighters. Keep them safe as they fight fires. Amen.

The men in Daniel 3 are not firefighters but they are put into a fire. Who rescues them?

Talking on the phone

Milly's aunt lives a long way away, so Milly doesn't see her aunt very often. But they love talking on the telephone. We can't see God, but we can talk to him whenever we want and we don't even need a telephone! We can pray. We can talk to God out loud or quietly to ourselves. God loves to talk with us.

PRAYER FOR TODAY

I'm glad I can talk to you, dear God, any time, night or day. Thanks for always listening, when I stop to pray. Amen.

What are Samuel and God talking about in today's story? Find out in 1 Samuel 16:1–13.

Beware! Tigers!

The sign outside the tiger's cage says "KEEP OUT." The zookeepers know that tigers can be dangerous. They don't want us to get hurt, so they put the sign there to warn us. God warns us too. When he tells us not to do something, it is because he loves us and doesn't want us to get hurt.

When you're not sure what God wants you to do, pray David's prayer (Psalm 25:4–7).

PRAYER FOR TODAY
It's great that you love me so much, God. I know you don't want me to get hurt. Help me to do what you tell me. Amen.

Tigers in danger

I love striped tigers. There used to be hundreds of thousands of them but now there aren't many tigers left in the wild. Isn't that sad? God has given us a really important job. He wants us all to look after his world and care for all the animals, fish, and birds that he has made. Can you think of ways you could do that?

e Bible talks about
the important job
od has given us in
Genesis 1:26–28.

PRAYER FOR TODAY
Dear God, show me how
I can take care of your
wonderful world and all
the amazing animals you
have made.
Amen.

A rainbow

Have you ever seen a rainbow in the sky? Sam is painting a rainbow. He has heard the story of how God rescued Noah and the animals from a terrible flood. God put a rainbow in the sky as a promise that he would never flood the whole earth again. God keeps his promises!

PRAYER FOR TODAY
Dear God, you keep
your promises.
Thank you that
I can trust you.
Amen.

Read the amazing story of Noah and the ark in Genesis 7.

Like dad

David loves playing football with his dad. Do you think they look alike? David wants to be just like his dad when he grows up. He is his dad's special son. The Bible says that Jesus is God's special son. Jesus is just like his heavenly Father. He is loving and kind. God wants everyone to love Jesus.

PRAYER FOR TODAY
Dear God, thank you for sending your son, Jesus, to be my friend.
Amen.

Read what Jesus said about his heavenly Father in John 5:19–21.

Smiling

What makes you smile? Watching cartoons or reading my favorite joke book makes me smile. We smile at jokes or when we see someone we love. We smile when we do something we like or when someone is kind to us. We smile to say "hello" and "thank you." And when we remember how much God loves us, we smile and smile!

PRAYER FOR TODAY
Jesus, I smile because you're my friend, Jesus, you're with me, your love never ends. Amen.

We can always be glad we belong to Jesus. See Philippians 4:4.

feeling happy

How is Emily feeling today? How can you tell? Emily is smiling, so I think she is happy. Some people hum, whistle, or sing when they are happy. When something really good happens they might jump about, skip, dance, or shout to show how happy they are. What do you do when you are really happy?

PRAYER FOR TODAY
Dear God,
I sing and shout to show you how glad I am to know you!
Amen.

God likes it when we shout for joy! Read Psalm 68:3.

Harvest festival

Let's celebrate harvest time! Farmers work really hard to grow and gather in the crops. At harvest time we offer back to God some of the good things he gives us and we thank him. People often take food or money to church to give to people who don't have enough. How will you celebrate the harvest?

PRAYER FOR TODAY
Dear God, thank you for all the good things you give me. Help me to share them with others. Amen.

Joseph shares the harvest wisely in Egypt. Read Genesis 41:47–57.

Can you smell it?

God gave you your nose. It doesn't matter if it is big or small, wide or thin, straight, curved, or pointed. God made it specially for smelling. Your nose can tell you if something is good to eat or not. It can smell smoke to warn you of dangerous fires. We love some smells and hate others! What smell do you like most?

There is a strong smell in today's story. Find out if it is a good or a bad smell in John 12:1–4.

PRAYER FOR TODAY
Thank you for my nose, God. I love the smell of

....
Amen.

Amazing birds

God has made all kinds of birds. He made big birds and tiny birds. He made some with very long necks and others with very big beaks. Some birds can fly, some can walk, and some can swim. Can you spot the different birds in the picture? What are their names? Can you find the bird that can't fly at all?

PRAYER FOR TODAY
Wow, God, the birds you have made are so many different shapes and sizes! It's amazing! My favorite is the

....
Amen.

Read Genesis 1:20–21 to find out what God thinks about the birds he has made.

where do they live?

When God made the world he made sure there were places for all his birds to live and lots of food for them to eat. Can you guess where these birds live? Do they live in hot or cold countries? What do you think they like to eat?

PRAYER FOR TODAY
Dear God, it's great you love everything you have made. Thank you for giving us all somewhere to live and food to eat. Amen.

Read Matthew 6:25–26 to find out what Jesus says about God, the birds, and us.

Mixing colors is great fun!

Sally is learning all about mixing colors, with some help from her teacher. Who helps you to learn new things? God helps us learn in many different ways and places. Think about where you can learn things this week.

PRAYER FOR TODAY

Dear God, thank you for all the people who teach me, especially

....

Amen.

Daniel goes to school in a king's court! Find out what he learns in Daniel 1:3–17.

Healthy teeth

Have you been to the dentist recently ? The dentist looks carefuly into your mouth and checks that all your teeth are healthy. The dentist tells you how to clean your teeth and to eat food that is good for teeth. What do you need to clean your teeth?

PRAYER FOR TODAY

Thank you, God, for all my teeth. Thank you for dentists who help me take care of them. Amen.

Which of Jacob's twelve sons has sparkling teeth? Find out in Genesis 49:8–12.

Names

As soon as this baby was born, his mom and dad gave him a name. He is called Harrison George Parker. But his mom and dad call him Harry for short. God knows you by name: he knows your first name, your last name, even your middle names. And if you have a nickname, he knows that, too! You are really special to him.

PRAYER FOR TODAY
There's lots of names that I could be,
I thank you, God, that I am me.
Amen.

Find out what name is given to the baby in today's Bible story. Read Luke 1:57–66.

Baptism

Have you ever been to a baby's christening, baptism, or dedication? It is a special church service to thank God for a new baby. At Harry's baptism, Harry's parents thanked God for their baby and promised God they would teach Harry about Jesus. The whole church welcomed Harry into God's family.

Today's story is about Jesus' dedication service. See Luke 2:22–33.

PRAYER FOR TODAY
Dear God, it's great to belong to your family. Thank you for the people who tell me about you. Amen.

Ruining things

Rosa is angry. Amy has ruined her painting. When someone spoils our work, we might want to shout at them, push them away, or destroy their work too. God asks us to love our friends and forgive them even when they have done something mean to us. What do you think Rosa should do?

PRAYER FOR TODAY
Lord Jesus, it's so hard to be kind when someone ruins my things. You are always kind, help me to be like you. Amen.

Peter wants to know how many times he has to forgive his brother. Read Matthew 18:21–22 and find out what Jesus says.

"I'm sorry"

Amy has made her friend Rosa angry and sad. I think Amy should say she's sorry, don't you? Sometimes we don't want to apologize, even when we know we have done something wrong. And sometimes we say "I'm sorry" quickly, but we don't really mean it. When we are really sorry, we don't do the same unkind things again.

PRAYER FOR TODAY
Dear Jesus, I know I should say "I'm sorry" when I've upset someone. Help me to say it and mean it.
Amen.

Jesus tells us it is very important to say "I'm sorry" and make things right. See Matthew 5:23–26.

Playing with friends

Playing is so much more fun when you have friends. Who do you like to play with? Trent and Joel love playing all sorts of games together. Sometimes they play "let's pretend" games, sometimes they play with Joel's train set, but today they are playing with Trent's bricks. God is glad when we share our toys and play kindly with our friends.

PRAYER FOR TODAY
Dear God, thank you for my friend

....
Please help us to play well together. Amen.

If you want to find out how God wants you to play with your friends. Read 1 Thessalonians 5:15

working together

Trent and Joel love building towers. Sometimes they fight over who has the most blocks but today they want to build a really tall tower, so they are working together. They are taking turns to put blocks on top. I think their tower will be finished soon. What a good idea it is to work together!

PRAYER FOR TODAY
Dear God, it's fun working together with my friends. I am sorry I fight with them sometimes.
Amen.

Long ago, many different people worked together to build something. Find out what they built in Nehemiah 2 and 3.

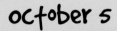

Listening to others

Who is good at listening to you? At Amy's nursery school they have "show and tell." Amy likes taking her special things. Everyone listens quietly as she tells them her news. She is showing her class this picture she has painted for her grandmother, who is in the hospital. What would you take for "show and tell?"

PRAYER FOR TODAY
Thank God for the people who listen to you.
Dear God, thank you for

....

He/she is good at listening to me.
Amen.

In today's story, Philip shares his news. Who is listening to him? Are they good listeners? Find out in Acts 8:5–8.

Helping others

Rachel thinks it's great being a big girl! She helps to dress her baby sister, she picks up the toys Sarah throws out of the stroller, and she sings to her. Can you think of other ways of showing love and helping little children? Baby Sarah can't say "thank you" yet, but she does give Rachel big smiles!

Find out how Miriam helps her baby brother. See Exodus 2:1–10.

PRAYER FOR TODAY

Now I'm getting bigger, Jesus, please help me to take good care of little children, especially

....

Amen.

Good friends

Friends are great, aren't they? I'm glad God has given me such good friends. We talk about all sorts of things and share our news. Do you have a friend you like to talk to? What do you talk about?

PRAYER FOR TODAY
Dear God, thank you for friends to talk to. Thank you especially for my friend

....

Amen.

In today's story, Jesus makes some new friends. They spend all day talking! See John 1:35–39.

Your best friend

Did you know that Jesus is your best friend? You can tell him anything! Whether you are sad, happy, crabby, scared, or tired, Jesus will always listen to you. He will never leave you or say he doesn't want to be your friend. He is always by your side so you are never alone.

PRAYER FOR TODAY
Jesus, I love you. Thank you for being such a great friend. Amen.

Nobody liked Zacchaeus. But one day he made a new friend. Read Luke 19:1–10.

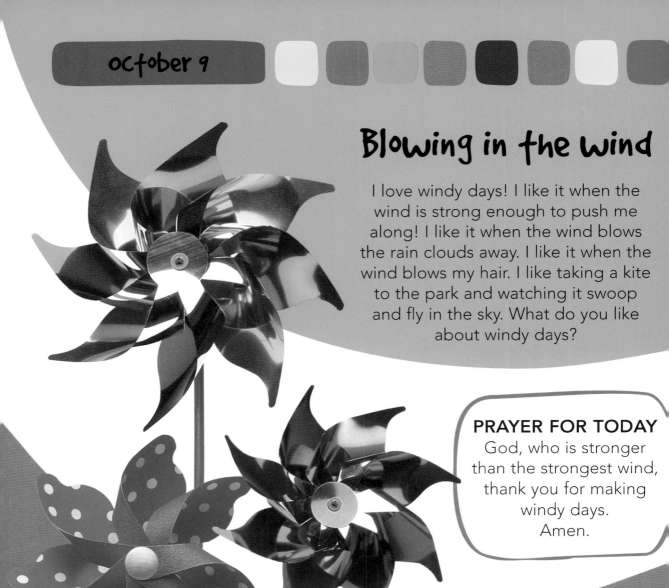

Blowing in the wind

I love windy days! I like it when the wind is strong enough to push me along! I like it when the wind blows the rain clouds away. I like it when the wind blows my hair. I like taking a kite to the park and watching it swoop and fly in the sky. What do you like about windy days?

PRAYER FOR TODAY
God, who is stronger than the strongest wind, thank you for making windy days.
Amen.

Not all windy days are fun. In today's story, Jesus shows that he is stronger than the wind. Read Mark 4:35–41.

Have a drink!

Imagine it's a really hot day. You have been playing outside in the sun and now you're really, really thirsty! What would you like to drink? Sometimes water tastes best of all! But in some countries there is no clean water to drink. Next time you have a drink, whisper "thank you" to God for it!

PRAYER FOR TODAY
Dear God, thank you for all my different drinks.
Amen.

In today's story, Jesus helps to provide drinks at a big wedding! Read John 2:1–10.

Party clothes

Lydia is excited. I wonder if you can guess where she is going. She has chosen her favorite clothes and they have been cleaned and ironed specially for today. Lydia is going to a party! What do you do to get ready for a party? What do you like to wear?

PRAYER FOR TODAY

Lord God, I like parties! They're fun! It's exciting getting ready to go. My favorite party clothes are

....

Thank you for my nice clothes. Amen.

Jesus tells a story about a king's special party. What do the people wear to the party? Find out in Matthew 22:1–14.

Paint a present

Ying is painting a special picture. It's going to be for her grandma. Ying loves her grandma so much! And her grandma loves the things Ying makes. Who do you make special things for? Can you think of anything God has made just for you?

PRAYER FOR TODAY
Dear God, please bless

....
today. I love him/her
so much.
Amen.

Jacob gives his son Joseph a special present. Find out what it is in Genesis 37:3.

A book of stories

Milly loves looking at her Bible. It is full of great stories. There are exciting stories, like the story of how God made the world. There are sad stories, like the story of Adam and Eve disobeying God. But the most wonderful story is about Jesus who came to make us friends with God again.

PRAYER FOR TODAY
Thank you, God, for the Bible.
Thank you for

....,
who tells me the stories of Jesus.
Amen.

There are so many stories about Jesus! Today's story shows us how powerful Jesus is. Read Mark 6:45–52.

God's friends

The Bible is the best book ever! It tells us what God is like. It tells us how much he loves us and how he wants us to be his friends. And as we read the stories of the Bible, we also learn how to be good friends to God.

PRAYER FOR TODAY
Dear God, it's amazing that you want to be friends with me! I want to learn to be a good friend to you.
Amen.

As we read the Bible, God shows us how he wants us to live. See Psalm 119:105.

feeling angry

Sometimes our friends upset us when they say mean things to us or won't let us play with them. When we are upset, we start crying or we may get angry and say something mean back. Jesus said that when someone does something mean to us, we must not be mean to them. Instead Jesus wants us to be kind to them.

PRAYER FOR TODAY
Jesus, it's hard to be kind when someone has been mean to me. Please help me. Amen.

What should you do when someone is unkind to you? Read Matthew 5:39–42.

forgiving

Zac has taken Daniel's vacuum cleaner and won't give it back. It looks like Daniel is very upset. What do you think Zac should do? I think he is ready to say he's sorry. What do you think Daniel should do then? He could shake hands with Zac to show he forgives his friend or he could share his vacuum cleaner and take turns with Zac.

PRAYER FOR TODAY
Dear Jesus, when my friends upset me, please help me to forgive them. Amen.

God has forgiven us, which is why he wants us to forgive others. See Colossians 3:13.

The doctor

Sometimes when we are ill, we need to see a doctor. God has given doctors the important job of figuring out what is wrong with our bodies. Doctors spend a long time learning about how God has made us. They know which medicines will help us get better quickly.

PRAYER FOR TODAY
Lord God, thank you for giving us doctors to care for us when we are ill. Please help them with their work.
Amen.

Jesus was the best doctor of all. He made people better without any medicine! Read Matthew 4:23–24.

Worrying

Did you know that God loves you so much he wants to help you when you are worried? Worrying can make us feel sad or out of sorts. We may worry about starting school or going to a new play group. We may get worried when it gets dark or when we have to walk past a barking dog. Talk to God about the things that worry you.

PRAYER FOR TODAY

Hello God, I get worried about

....

It makes me feel

....

When I feel like that, please help me. Amen.

When you get worried, remember what Peter wrote to his friends. Read 1 Peter 5:7.

"Thank you!"

A present! How exciting! I wonder what it is? I hope the children will remember to say "thank you!" The Bible tells us to keep on saying "thank you" to God for all that he gives us. What will you thank God for today?

PRAYER FOR TODAY
Thank you, God, for all your good gifts. Today I thank you for

....

Amen.

Psalm 136 is a song of thanks. Use verses 1–9, 23–26 to help you with your prayer.

Jesus taught his friends a special prayer. You can find it in Matthew 6:9–13.

Talking to God

Prayer is talking to God. It doesn't matter whether we talk to God with our eyes shut or our eyes open. It doesn't matter if we are standing up, sitting down, lying in our beds, or kneeling. We can talk to God anywhere and everywhere. We can talk to him out loud and quietly in our heads. He loves to talk with us.

PRAYER FOR TODAY
Dear God, I know I can talk to you about anything. I know you are my loving heavenly Father, who always listens. I want to tell you about

....

Amen.

Let's imagine!

God has given us sharp minds to imagine all sorts of things. We use our imagination every day. Sometimes Olivia pretends she's a fairy, sometimes she's a princess, but today she's imagining being grown-up like her mom. What do you like to imagine?

PRAYER FOR TODAY
Thank you, God, for giving me my imagination.
Amen.

Isaiah 65:17–25 helps us imagine what God's new world will be like.

Dressing up

Olivia loves dressing up in her mom's clothes. She wants to be just like her mom when she's grown up. Who do you want to be like? God is our Father and he wants us to be like him. We can't dress up to look like God but we can be kind and loving to everyone, just like he is.

PRAYER FOR TODAY
Dear God, help me to grow up to be like you. Amen.

Find out more about God in Luke 6:35–36.

Sharing with others

God is good at sharing! He has made a world full of wonderful things to share with us. He wants us to share what we have with others. What is Jan sharing with Lydia today? What do you have that you can share with others?

PRAYER FOR TODAY
Lord God, you're a sharing God, a caring God, a kind and giving God. Help me to be sharing, caring, kind and giving, just like you! Amen.

Read Isaiah 58:7 to find out what God says about sharing.

our homes

God gives us homes to keep us safe. Our homes are all different. My home is cool and shady in the summer, when it's hot. It is warm, dry, and cozy in the winter, when it's not. It's full of books and cuddly toys. It's sometimes messy and there's lots of noise! What's your home like?

PRAYER FOR TODAY
Thank you for my home, God. I like it because

....
Amen.

Everybody wants to get into the house where Jesus is staying. Some people even make a hole in the roof so that they can get in! Read Mark 2:1–5.

clothes

What are you wearing today? A woolly sweater or woolly socks? Or maybe a cotton T-shirt or jeans? Everything we wear comes from the wonderful world God has made. God made sheep that give us wool to make warm sweaters and socks. God made the cotton plant that gives us cotton to make into T-shirts and jeans. What a kind and loving God we have!

PRAYER FOR TODAY
Thank you, loving God, for clothes to keep me warm in winter and cool in summer. Amen.

God cares for us so much that he makes sure we have clothes to wear. See Matthew 6:28–30.

caring and giving

God wants us to be caring, giving people. We can even give clothes to others who need them. The clothes that are too small for you might fit your younger brother or sister. And if your brother or sister doesn't need them, you can give them away to someone who does!

PRAYER FOR TODAY
Dear God, please take care of all the people who don't have clothes. Show me how I can help them. Amen.

When we help others we show Jesus that we love him. Read Matthew 25:31–40.

Splashing in the water

Do you like diving under the water and being splashed? Milly does! She's wet from head to toe! Sophie loves playing in the water but she hates being splashed. She doesn't like getting water in her eyes. They have had great fun together because Milly has been very careful not to splash Sophie. What a kind friend!

PRAYER FOR TODAY
Tell Jesus what you like and what you don't like about playing in the water.
Jesus, the best/worst thing about playing in the water is

....
Amen.

Even the sailors are scared of the water in today's story. Read Jonah 1:1–17.

Swimming

Sophie and Milly like swimming. At the swimming pool, Sophie wears her armbands but she doesn't need them to have fun in the wading pool! Today the two friends have been jumping in and out, finding things that float and kicking the water out! Do you like swimming or playing in the water? What do you like best?

PRAYER FOR TODAY
Thank you, God, for water,
it's fun to play and swim.
If you hear a great big
SPLASH,
it's just ME jumping in!
Amen.

Today's story is about a special pool in Jerusalem. People didn't go there to swim, they went to get well! Find out more in John 5:1–9.

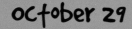

Fighting

Do you ever fight with your brother or sister? When you're mad at them, or they're mad at you, you can end up hitting, pinching, calling each other names, or taking each other's toys. God doesn't want you to hurt each other. He loves everyone in your family.

PRAYER FOR TODAY
I'm sorry when I argue and fight,
help me to love and to do what's right.
Amen.

Even though the brothers in today Bible story are me to each other, Go loves them all. See Genesis 37:1– 12–28 and 50:15–

Loving people

What do you do if someone starts to argue or fight with you? Does it make you really angry or does it make you feel sad and lonely? Lots of people wanted to pick a fight with Jesus. But Jesus did something amazing! Instead of fighting back, he loved them! Jesus wants us to be like him. It's not easy but he will help us.

PRAYER FOR TODAY
Dear Jesus, I want to love people, like you did. Please help me. Amen.

Find out what Jesus says you should do if someone is mean to you. Read Luke 6:35–36.

Amazing eyes

Look around you! What can you see? Can you see something blue? Can you see something round? God has made a world with all sorts of colors and shapes. And he has given us eyes to see it all. Isn't God great?

PRAYER FOR TODAY
Thank you, God,
for eyes to see,
thank you, God,
for making me!
Amen.

In today's story, Jesus helps two men to see again. Read Matthew 20:29–34.

Look at your eyes!

Find a mirror and look very carefully at your eyes. What color are they? Are they black, blue, brown, green, or a different color in between? Do you have long eyelashes or short eyelashes, narrow eyes or round eyes? God has made us all different. He likes the way he has made us. We are special to him.

PRAYER FOR TODAY

Thank you, God, for giving me lovely

....

eyes. I'm glad I can see your world.
Amen.

Psalm 66:5 encourages us to use our eyes to see how great God is.

Nurses

Nurses are very caring people. They work with doctors to take care of us. When we fall and cut ourselves badly, they clean the wound and bandage us up. They give us injections to stop us from getting really ill. Can you think of other ways nurses make you feel better?

PRAYER FOR TODAY
Dear God, thank you for nurses who work so hard to take care of us. Amen.

Jesus tells a story about a man from Samaria who is like a nurse. Read Luke 10:30–35.

Working together

PRAYER FOR TODAY
Dear God, please help me to listen to my friends when they have good ideas. Amen.

What can we make together? Cassie has got a really good idea. Aisha knows a lot about building. Max has counted out the number of bricks they need. Together they can make a really strong tower. It's great fun, working as a team! God sometimes puts us together with friends to work as a team for him.

Jesus chose twelve special friends to help him. Find out who they are in Matthew 9:9–13.

A strong tower

Joel's last tower wobbled and fell down, so he has started again. What would you do to stop your tower from falling down? This time Joel is building his tower on a good strong surface. Jesus said that life is like building a tower. If we want to have good, strong lives we should do what he says.

PRAYER FOR TODAY
Dear Jesus, thank you for the Bible that tells us what you want us to do. Please help me to do what you say.
Amen.

Jesus tells a story about building. You can find it in Luke 6:46–49.

fingerprints

This baby is different from every other baby. And you are different from every other boy or girl right down to your fingertips. If you have ever done finger painting, you will know that each of your fingerprints is different. God made every bit of you. You are very precious to him. There is nobody else like you!

Psalm 139 is a song about God making us, loving us, and knowing all about us.

PRAYER FOR TODAY
How wonderful to be made by you and loved by you, dear God! Amen.

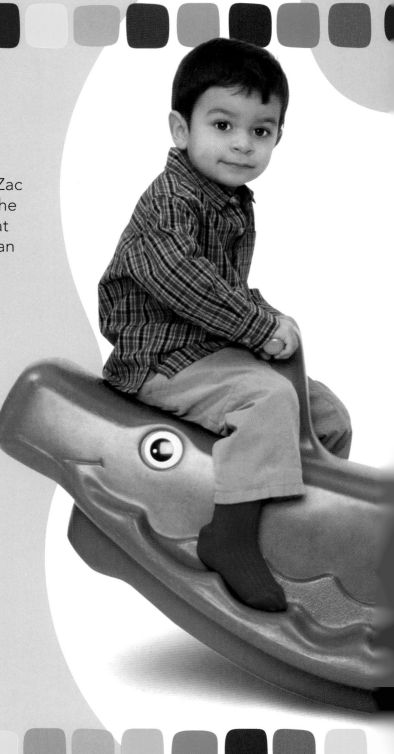

Having fun

Up and down, up and down! Zac and Anna are having fun on the seesaw. Isn't it wonderful that God gives us friends so we can have fun playing together? What games do you play with your friends?

PRAYER FOR TODAY
Dear God, I have fun playing with

....
Thank you for my friend. Amen.

Read Acts 2:44–47 to find out what Jesus' friends do together.

Helping each other

Have you ever tried to seesaw on your own? It doesn't work very well. In fact, it's no fun at all! But when you have a friend helping on the other end you can seesaw as much as you like. It's fun when we play together and help each other.

PRAYER FOR TODAY
Jesus, you help me every day, help me to help my friends, I pray. Amen.

Paul writes to his friends in Rome to ask them to help another friend of his. Who is she? Read Romans 16:1–2 to find out!

Families

How many people are there in your family? Do you know how many people there are in God's family? Too many to count! God's family is made up of all the people who love him and know that God loves them too. In God's family we can sing and dance, and we can find out how much he loves us!

PRAYER FOR TODAY
Dear God, thank you that I can belong to your family!
That's great!
Amen.

There's a song in the Bible about being in God's family. Look today at Psalm 133.

Singing

What is your favorite song? Do you know any songs about God? God loves to hear us sing to him. It doesn't matter if you can't sing in tune or if you forget the words. God loves to hear you. If you sing with others, it can make a fantastic sound!

PRAYER FOR TODAY
Dear God, I want to sing, I want to shout, and praise you!
Amen.

See which instruments you can find in Psalm 150, then say the last verse out loud!

Talking to God

God loves us and takes care of us all through the day, so it is good to talk to him at night before we go to sleep. We can tell him all about the fun we've had, what we've done, and what we've learned. We can say we're sorry for the things we did wrong and ask him to help us tomorrow.

PRAYER FOR TODAY
Dear God, thank you for today. I liked doing

.... I'm sorry for ....
Please help me tomorrow.
Amen.

At night, we can sing and pray to God about all he has given us in the day. See Psalm 42:8.

A favorite teddy

This very cuddly teddy is called Bertie. He is Molly's favorite toy and they go everywhere together. One day, Molly lost Bertie and was very sad. She asked God to help her find Bertie. And he did! Do you have a favorite toy? Is it a teddy, like Bertie, or is it something else?

PRAYER FOR TODAY
Dear God, thank you for all my toys. But thank you especially for

....
Amen.

Jesus tells a story about a woman who loses something very precious. What is it? Read Luke 15:8–10.

Teeth

Teeth are important! If you didn't have teeth, you wouldn't be able to eat anything crunchy or chewy. Milly's two wobbly front teeth have come out. Her new big teeth are growing slowly. Milly is taking good care of her new teeth. She brushes them carefully and doesn't eat too many sweets. How many teeth do you have? How do you look after them?

PRAYER FOR TODAY
Thank you, God,
for teeth to bite, to crunch and munch and chew, I'll keep them bright and clean and white, to last my whole life through.
Amen.

God made every part of us, even our teeth! See Psalm 139:13.

Visiting grandpa

Chloe's grandpa has not been very well. He has been in the hospital so Chloe has come to visit him. Grandpa is very happy to see her. Jesus is also pleased when we care for people who are sick. And he is glad when we cheer them up. Do you know someone in hospital or someone who isn't very well?

PRAYER FOR TODAY
Talk to God about someone you know who isn't well.
Dear God, please help

....

to get better. Amen.

Find out what Jesus says about people who care for others. Read Matthew 25:31–40.

Singing

I think God must like music because when he made us he gave us a special instrument. You carry it with you wherever you go. Can you guess what it is? Yes, a voice! We can sing or hum wherever we are – in the bath, in the playground, in bed, and in the car! What's your favorite song? You could sing it to God now!

PRAYER FOR TODAY
I like music, too, God. I'm glad you gave me a voice to sing. Thank you.

Even if you don't want to sing, you can praise God in lots of other ways. Look at Psalm 150.

Jumping

One, two, three, JUMP! Jumping is fun. How high can you jump? If you didn't have legs you wouldn't be able to jump. What else can you do with your legs? Can you balance on one leg? What about hopping, skipping, kicking, and dancing? What a good thing God gave us legs!

PRAYER FOR TODAY
Thank you for my legs, God, I can jump so high! One, two, three, watch me jump up to the sky! Amen.

Today's story is about a man whose legs don't work. Find out what happens to him in Acts 3:1–10.

Cooking

Sam is helping his mom cook a meal. He has cracked some eggs into his bowl, and added flour, milk, and a bit of salt. What do you think he is making? Pancakes! Have you ever made pancakes? It's lots of fun! Isn't God amazing to give us so many different kinds of food to enjoy?

PRAYER FOR TODAY

Thank you, dear God, for the fun I have when I cook, especially when I help make

....

Amen.

Jesus and his friends made a special meal together in Luke 22:7–13. Find out what it was called.

Helping mom

Does your mom sometimes ask you to help? If you're busy playing, it can be difficult to stop and do what she asks. But sometimes it's more fun helping than playing! You can be a good helper, too, if your mom is very busy. Ask God to show you how you can help at home today!

PRAYER FOR TODAY
Dear God, make me ready to help today and show me what I can do. Amen.

Sarah helped Abraham make a special meal in Genesis 18:1–9. What did they cook?

Feeling scared

If you sometimes feel scared, try to remember that God is always with you. Tell him about it. There's nothing too scary for God! Sometimes it's difficult to say why you are scared, but you feel all shaky inside. Close your eyes and imagine that Jesus is with you, giving you a hug. You are always safe with him.

PRAYER FOR TODAY
Dear God, please be with me when I feel scared, especially

....
Amen.

Psalm 121:5–8 says that God will always protect us. Read it out loud.

Money

Milly and Rachel are playing store. They are using play money. Do you have some money of your own – maybe pocket money or birthday money? It can be hard deciding whether to spend it or save it in your piggy bank. God wants us to be wise and kind with the money we have. Can you think of ways you can be kind with your money?

PRAYER FOR TODAY

Dear God, thank you for the money that I have. Please help me to spend it well. Amen.

Jesus tells his friends how to spend their money well. See Luke 12:32–34.

An amazing universe

Did you know that God made the universe so huge it would take 15 billion years to travel from one end to the other? That's a very long time! Then God made the stars. They look small to us but they are actually huge balls of burning gas. They look small because they are so far away. What an amazing universe God has made!

PRAYER FOR TODAY
The universe is so, so huge,
and I am so, so small.
The stars are bright,
to give us light.
Thanks, God, You made it all!
Amen.

Genesis 1:14–19 tells the story of God making the sun, the moon and the stars.

The moon and stars

We don't have street lights where I live. At night it is really dark. On cloudy nights, I need my flashlight to see where I'm going. But on clear nights, the moon and the stars light up my way. Stars can even help you find your way again when you are lost. How good of God to make the moon and the stars!

PRAYER FOR TODAY
For the beauty of the night,
for the moon that gives us light,
for the stars that shine so bright,
we thank you, God.
Amen.

In today's story, a star helps a group of people to find someone very special. Read Matthew 2:1–10.

Let me drive!

Ben is upset and angry because Josh won't let him have a turn at driving. When someone has been unkind to us, we feel like hurting them, too, by hitting, pinching, or calling them names. But Jesus wants us to love them instead. It is hard to do, but Jesus will help us to be kind and loving.

PRAYER FOR TODAY
Dear Jesus, it's hard to be kind when someone is mean to me. Please help me to be loving. Amen.

Find out what Jesus says we should do when someone is mean to us. See Matthew 5:43–45.

Being kind

Melanie knows that Josh is not being very kind to Ben. She can see that Ben is feeling sad. What do you think Melanie could do to make Ben feel better and to stop Josh from being unkind? When we see others being teased in the playground, or left out of games at home, Jesus wants us to be kind.

PRAYER FOR TODAY
Dear Jesus, please show me when others are feeling sad or hurt and help me to be kind. Amen.

People want to hurt Paul in today's story. Find out how Paul's friends help him. See Acts 9:23–25.

A broken toy

Have you ever had a really special toy that got broken? How did you feel? Could it be fixed? Isn't it a great feeling when something is mended again? God knows exactly how you feel when you are upset. And he is happy for you when things are fixed!

PRAYER FOR TODAY
Dear God, I'm really happy when things can be fixed. Thank you!
Amen.

Nehemiah rebuilds the broken walls of the city. How do the people thank God in Nehemiah 12:43?

Enjoy your books!

Reading books is fun! You can read exciting stories. You can find out what happened long ago. You can discover wonderful things about the world God has made – from planets to plants and rockets to rainbows. And when you read God's special book, the Bible, you learn about God.

PRAYER FOR TODAY
Thank you for all my books, God. But most of all, thank you for the Bible that tells me about you. Amen.

The Bible says that Jesus came to show us what God is like. Read John 14:6–11.

Land and sea

When God created the world, it was covered in water. Then he told the waters to move to make room for dry land and they did! Isn't God amazing? If you look at a globe or a map, you can figure out where the land is and where the oceans are.

PRAYER FOR TODAY
Wow, God you are awesome!
What a great idea to make the
land and the sea!
Amen.

Read how God made the
land and the seas in
Genesis 1:9–10.

Where do you live?

Can you find where you live on a map or a globe? Olivia and Trent live in a country that is surrounded by sea. God made every country in the world. He made some with high mountains, others with green hills or deep canyons, long beaches or rocky shores. The world was God's idea and all of it belongs to him.

PRAYER FOR TODAY
Tell God what you like about the place where you live.
You've made a fantastic world, God!
I like

....

because

....

Amen.

Psalm 95:3–5 is a Bible song about God's world. Why not make up a tune for it!

Caring for pets

God's creatures all have their special homes. Birds nest in trees and rabbits burrow in the hills. Even our pets have special places. Cats nap in their baskets. The hamster scurries around in its cage. The fish swim round the tank. We can take care of our pets by keeping their special homes safe and clean.

PRAYER FOR TODAY
Cleaning out cages is a messy job, God. I'm sorry when I make a fuss. Please help me do it well.
Amen.

Psalm 104:16–18 tells us about the homes of some of God's wild creatures.

Clean-up time!

It's really fun playing with the big puzzle pieces at preschool. But now Archie has to put them all away. I think he wants to keep playing but he knows that everything must be cleaned up before story time. Are you good at cleaning up? What things do you put away at school?

Read John 6:5–13 and find out what Jesus' friends have to clean up.

PRAYER FOR TODAY
I've played with all the toys, God,
they're scattered on the floor,
I know it's time to pick them up,
But.........can't I play some more?
Amen.

Unkind words

Sometimes when Melanie and Ben play together they argue and say mean things to each other. Melanie gets upset when Ben says something unkind to her. And Ben gets upset when Melanie says horrible things to him. God does not want us to upset one another, that's why God wants Melanie and Ben to use kind words and be friendly.

PRAYER FOR TODAY
Dear God, I'm sorry for arguing and not being friendly to others. Please help me to use kind words to everyone. Amen.

Psalm 19:14 is a prayer asking God to help us speak as he wants us to.

Lots to do!

There is so much to do at preschool! Melanie and Ben can play in the home corner or the sandpit. They can choose to play with the modeling clay, the building blocks, or the farm set. Can you see what they have chosen today? What do you choose to do at school?

PRAYER FOR TODAY

I like to go to school, God,
there's lots to make and do,
there's lots of fun and playtime,
so much for me to choose.
Amen.

In today's story, two men choose different places to build their houses. Find out what happens in Matthew 7:24–27.

Taking care of the world

Yuck! What a mess! What a horrible smell! God has given us a beautiful world to live in. He made grown-ups and children, and asked us to care for his world. He wants us to look after it properly. Can you think of ways you can do that?

PRAYER FOR TODAY
Dear God, thank you for giving us a beautiful world to live in. Help us to take care of it. Amen.

Today's story is about God giving people his world to look after. Read Genesis 1:26–31.

A smelly mess!

The world and everything in it belongs to God. That means we have to look after it very carefully. When we drop plastic wrappers or cans, it makes God's world messy and makes it dangerous for birds and animals that might choke on the trash. We must all work together to take care of God's world.

PRAYER FOR TODAY
Dear Lord God, we're so sorry for messing up your wonderful world. Please forgive us and teach us to take better care of it. Amen.

Psalm 24:1 reminds us that the world does not belong to us.

Sharing

Have you ever had friends over to play at your house? Or maybe you have had people who have come for dinner or to stay overnight? It's exciting having visitors! It's fun to share our toys, our food, and our homes with others. It makes God happy, too, because he shares everything he has made with us!

PRAYER FOR TODAY
Dear God, thank you for giving me so much. Help me to be like you and share my home and my toys with others. Amen.

The woman in today's story shares her home. Find out more in 2 Kings 4:8–17.

Welcome!

Zac loves having visitors. If you knocked on the door of his playhouse, he would open it and invite you in. He would let you sit on his chair and he would make you a drink and let you play with him. When we welcome people and make them feel special, we are being like God, because God thinks everybody is special. He is ready to welcome us all.

PRAYER FOR TODAY
God welcomes me,
he welcomes you,
and makes us welcoming
people, too.
Amen.

Read Genesis 18:1–8 and find out who Abraham welcomes to his home.

Where food comes from

Think of your favorite food. Do you know where it comes from? This fruit comes from many countries round the world. Oranges need a lot of sunshine to grow big and juicy. Apple trees need sun but enough rain, too. Isn't God amazing to make so many different fruits for us to enjoy?

PRAYER FOR TODAY
Crunchy, juicy, tangy and sweet,
Thank you, God, for the
fruit I eat!
Amen.

Look at Psalm 104:13–14 and think about where our food comes from.

Share it!

Look at this plate of fruit! Would it be fair if Sally ate all of it? What about the others? How can they share it fairly? God gives us so many good things to enjoy. He wants us to share them with others. What can you share with someone today?

PRAYER FOR TODAY
Help me, dear God, to share the things I like best. Amen.

Jesus says that God is kind to everybody. Read Matthew 5:43–48.

Taking turns

"I want to go first!" If everybody said that, there would be a big argument! There are some games that just don't work very well if we all try to play at the same time. Can you think of games where you and your friends have to take turns? Next time you play those games, practise letting your friend go first!

PRAYER FOR TODAY
Lord Jesus, it's hard to let others go first. Please help me to say "you go first," and to wait my turn. Amen.

In today's story Abraham lets his nephew Lot go first. Read Genesis 13:5–12.

Let me help!

Do you ever help your dad or grandpa? You may not be as tall or as skillful, but there are lots of things you can do to help. God has given us dads and grandfathers to help us learn so many things. What can you learn from yours?

PRAYER FOR TODAY
Dear God, thank you for

....,
who shows me
what to do.
Amen.

How does David help his father?
Read 1 Samuel 17:12–20.

Fed up!

It's hard to be good all the time, isn't it? Alice has just done something wrong. Her dad has scolded her and she has to sit quietly on the chair for a while. Alice hates that! Alice's dad isn't being mean. He loves Alice and he wants Alice to learn to be good.

PRAYER FOR TODAY
Dear God, I got it wrong again. I know I was naughty and I'm sorry. Please help me learn to be good.
Amen.

Our moms and dads teach us how God wants us to live. And God wants us to listen to them. Read Proverbs 6:20.

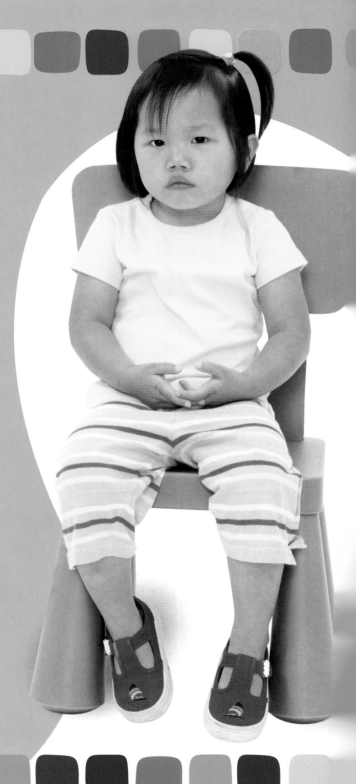

Lost

Louisa can't find her mommy. Have you ever been lost and not been able to find your mom or dad? How did you feel? Louisa is feeling frightened, lost, and alone. When you feel like that, remember that God is always with you. When you are frightened, talk to him because he wants to help you and take care of you.

PRAYER FOR TODAY
Dear God, thank you for loving me so much. If I get lost and frightened, please help me.
Amen.

Psalm 46:1 reminds us that God is always there to help us.

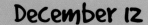

Whisper and shout!

We make all sorts of sounds with our voices.
We can talk and sing. We can whisper really
softly AND SHOUT REALLY LOUDLY. Maybe
you are good at shouting but are you as good
at whispering? Try it!

PRAYER FOR TODAY
Thank you, God, that I
can whisper,
THANK YOU, GOD,
THAT I CAN SHOUT!
Amen.

**In today's story, something
strange happens when
everybody shouts. What is it?
See Joshua 6:15–16,20.**

Listening

I wonder what Olivia is saying to her friend, George. George is listening carefully, so I think Olivia must be telling him something important. Jesus has lots of really important things to say to us, too. We need to listen carefully to him.

PRAYER FOR TODAY
Dear Jesus, help me to listen to what you say, then help me obey you, Lord, I pray.
Amen.

We can find out what Jesus wants to say to us in the Bible. Start by reading John 14:21.

Talking

Do you like to talk? It's fun to tell our best friends about all the exciting things we've done, and to share sad times, too. If something amazing has happened, who do you tell first? Do you tell your friends about the amazing things God does? Can you think of something you could tell them this week?

PRAYER FOR TODAY
Dear God, help me to tell my friends how much you love them, too. Amen.

In Luke 8:38–39, Jesus helps a man and tells him to talk to the whole town about it!

God Cares

God cares when your hamster dies. He cares when you fall off the swing. God cares when your favorite toy gets broken. And he knows how you feel when someone you love goes far away. No matter what happens, God cares for you.

PRAYER FOR TODAY
Tell God what you feel sad about.
Dear God, I know you care for me. Today, I feel sad about

....

Amen.

Poor Joseph was put into prison! But even in prison, God took care of him. Read Genesis 39:19–23.

Afraid of the dark

Emily is very tired, but she doesn't want to go to bed because she is scared of the dark. That's why she's holding her cuddly dog so tightly. Whenever we're afraid we can ask God to look after us. He has promised to protect us. God is more powerful than anyone or anything! And he's not afraid of the dark!

PRAYER FOR TODAY
Dear God, when I'm scared or can't get to sleep, help me to remember that you're always looking after me.
Amen.

**God has promised to take care of you.
Read Psalm 91:1–6.**

"Good night, God!"

It's time for stories, time for songs, time for hugs, time for bed! You snuggle under your covers, you shut your eyes, and you think of all the fun things you did today. It's time to say a "good night" prayer.

PRAYER FOR TODAY

I'm cozy, snuggled up in bed,
thoughts are running 'round my head.
Thank you, God, for my busy day,
keep me close to you, I pray.
Amen.

You can talk to God wherever you are, even lying in your bed! See Psalm 63:6–7.

car journeys

Traveling by car can be
dangerous, so there are special
chairs and belts to keep babies,
children, and grown-ups safe.
Can you think of other things
that are made to keep us safe?
God has promised that one day
he will come and live with us.
Then we will be safe from
danger and hurt forever.
Isn't that wonderful?

PRAYER FOR TODAY
Dear Jesus, keep me
safe from harm,
please hold me always
in your arms.
Amen.

Revelation 21:3–4 tells us
about the safe home we will
have with God one day.

Keeping promises

Sometimes we say things we shouldn't. We tell lies, we don't always keep our promises. But God never lies. What he says is true and he always keeps his promises. God wants us to learn to tell the truth and keep promises just as he does.

PRAYER FOR TODAY
Dear God, I'm sorry for telling lies. Please help me to tell the truth. Amen.

Find out what God hates and what pleases him in Proverbs 12:22.

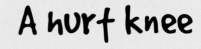

A hurt knee

Max has fallen down and hurt his knee again! That's the second time today. The first time, Max was at school. He tried to be brave. This time he is at home. He's glad his mom can pick him up and give him a big hug! God gives us special people to help us when we are hurt. Who helps you?

PRAYER FOR TODAY
Trip, crash, bang,
I've hurt my knee!
Thanks for

...................................,
who rescued me!
Amen.

In today's story, a kind person helps a wounded man. Read Luke 10:30–37.

Snow!

I'm glad God thought of making snow, aren't you? It's so much fun! You can ski on it, sled on it, build snowmen with it, and have great snowball fights! But it's cold and wet! What do you wear to keep warm and dry so you can have fun in the snow?

PRAYER FOR TODAY

I love to be out in the snow, God, it's fun to play and slide. Thank you for all my cozy clothes that keep me warm outside. Amen.

Psalm 148 is a song of praise to God. Even the snow joins in!

Wrapping presents

What kind of present would you like to be given? Would your dad like it too, or would he like something different? Buying presents for others is fun. We have to guess what the other person would like. And because God made us all so different, they don't always like what we like!

Today's story is about a queen who gives some very interesting presents. Read 1 Kings 10:1–10.

PRAYER FOR TODAY
Help me to think about others, God, and not always to think of what I want myself.
Amen.

Getting ready for Christmas

Only two days to go until Christmas! It's so exciting, but it's hard to wait! There are lots of things to do while we wait! We've put up the Christmas lights, we've decorated the Christmas tree, and wrapped the presents. What have you been doing to get ready for Christmas?

PRAYER FOR TODAY
Christmas is coming,
getting ready has been great.
Lord, help me to be patient,
'cause it's very hard to wait!
Amen.

The man in today's story has been waiting a long time and is very glad to see Jesus. Read about him in Luke 2:25–32.

God's present

Christmas began a long time ago when God gave the whole world a present. It wasn't a toy or a book or a puzzle. It was Jesus! When the little baby Jesus grew up, he rescued us so that we could be friends with God for ever. God must love us a lot to give us such a great present!

PRAYER FOR TODAY
Thank you, dear God, for loving me so much. Thank you for giving us Jesus. I'm so happy I can be your friend now. Amen.

God didn't wrap Jesus up, but he sent some special messengers to say that the present had arrived! Who were they? Find out in Luke 2:8–20.

A special celebration

It's Christmas! What an exciting day! We remember that God gave us Jesus – the best present ever! And today we say "thank you" to God for Jesus. Some people sing special Christmas songs. They have a party, eat Christmas food, and they give each other presents. What do you do to say "thank you" to God on Christmas Day?

PRAYER FOR TODAY
Christmas is exciting, God! Thank you for the fun, for presents, songs and special food, and Jesus Christ, your Son. Amen.

Jesus receives presents. Find out what they are in Matthew 2:1–2,9–11.

Christmas decorations

In some countries, there are Christmas concerts and plays to help people remember the story of the first Christmas. Christmas decorations also remind us of the day Jesus was born. Angels, stars, and gifts are all in the Christmas story. What decorations do you put up for Jesus' birthday?

PRAYER FOR TODAY
Stars and angels, party streamers and presents remind me that it's your birthday. Thank you, Lord Jesus, for Christmas time! Amen.

We have pictures of Jesus in a stable because the Bible says that Jesus slept in the animals' food trough. Read about it in Luke 2:1–7.

Christmas food

Christmas is Jesus' birthday. People all over the world celebrate Jesus' birthday with special party food. If you live in Portugal, you might eat salted fish. In Belgium they bake delicious spiced cookies. In England lots of people eat roast turkey and Christmas pudding. What special food do you eat at Christmas?

PRAYER FOR TODAY
Thank you, God, for delicious Christmas food. My favorite is

....
Amen.

God loves us and gives us good food. Read Psalm 145:8–9,15–16.

Snowflakes

Have you ever caught a snowflake?
Each one is beautiful. Every
snowflake has its own pattern and is
different from all the others. Isn't
that amazing! What a wonderful
world God has made!

PRAYER FOR TODAY
God in heaven, everything you
have made is good. Even
snowflakes show how
wonderful you are.
Amen.

**God makes the weather – the
ice, the frost, and the snow.
See Psalm 147:15–18.**

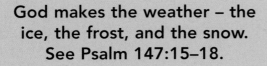

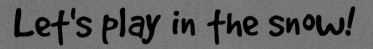

Let's play in the snow!

I've put on my thick coat, my hat, my gloves, my scarf and boots. I'm going to play in the snow. It's such fun making snowmen, throwing snowballs, skiing, and tobogganing. What do you like doing in the snow? I'm glad God made snow, aren't you?

PRAYER FOR TODAY
Snow is beautiful and it's fun, too! Thank you, God, for making snow.
Amen.

Psalm 148 is a song praising God for what he has made.

Going to the park

Do you like going to the park? I do! There are two parks where I live. One has green fields and a playground. The other has lakes and bridges and ducks to feed. Do you have a park or garden near you? What do you do there?

PRAYER FOR TODAY
Thank you, God, for parks.
I love to run about.
I swing and play and
feed the ducks,
I ride my bike and shout!
Amen.

Today's Bible story is about a garden where something very exciting happened. See John 19:41–20:18.

At the library

Have you ever chosen a book at a library? Libraries contain all kinds of books: story books and books of poems, books of things that happened long, long ago and books about how the world works. The Bible is like a library, too. It has real stories, made-up stories, songs, poems, and letters. You can choose a book from the Bible library every day!

PRAYER FOR TODAY
Thank you for all my books, Lord God. And thank you for your special book, the Bible. Amen.

Luke 8:4–8,11–15 is one of Jesus' stories.

Index of Bible readings

The Old Testament

Psalm 139:13–14 June 1
Psalm 139:14 April 19
Psalm 139:15–16 June 9
Psalm 139:1–6, 13–16 February 19
Psalm 139:7–10 September 8
Psalm 145:13 February 9
Psalm 145:8–9, 15–16 December 27
Psalm 147:15–18 December 28
Psalm 147:7–8 January 16
Psalm 147:7–9 May 31
Psalm 148 December 21, December 29
Psalm 148:11–13 April 10
Psalm 149:1–3 May 28
Psalm 150 July 28, November 9, November 14

Proverbs 12:22 December 19
Proverbs 13:1 August 24
Proverbs 18:10 July 6
Proverbs 6:20 December 10

Ecclesiastes 3:1–8 February 21

Isaiah 58:7 October 23
Isaiah 65:17–25 October 21

Jeremiah 18:1–4 February 11

Lamentations 3:22–24 January 3

Daniel 1 April 11
Daniel 1:3–17 September 27
Daniel 3 September 15
Daniel 6 April 29

Jonah 1:1–17 October 27
Jonah 1:1–4, 7, 11–12 March 13
Jonah 1:17 June 8

The New Testament

Matthew 1:18–25 September 7
Matthew 2:1–10 November 21
Matthew 2:1–2, 9–11 December 25
Matthew 2:9–12 August 8
Matthew 3:1–6 March 31
Matthew 4:18–22 September 13
Matthew 4:23–24 October 17
Matthew 5:23–26 October 2
Matthew 5:39–42 October 15
Matthew 5:42 August 4
Matthew 5:43–45 November 22
Matthew 5:43–48 December 7
Matthew 6:6–15 January 13
Matthew 6:9–13 October 20
Matthew 6:25–26 September 26
Matthew 6:28–30 October 25
Matthew 6:31–33 September 3
Matthew 7:12 May 13
Matthew 7:24–27 April 13, December 1
Matthew 9:9–13 November 3
Matthew 10:29–31 August 17
Matthew 13:1–9 April 12, May 21
Matthew 14:15–21 June 17
Matthew 18:21–22 October 1
Matthew 20:29–34 October 31
Matthew 21:1–11 March 22
Matthew 21:14–16 June 12
Matthew 22:1–14 July 18, October 11
Matthew 25:31–40 October 26, November 13
Matthew 26:7–13 September 9
Matthew 28:1–7 April 6
Matthew 28:8–10 April 7

Mark 1:29–31 June 10
Mark 1:30 May 18
Mark 1:32–34 May 19
Mark 1:35 January 1

John 19:16–18 and 28–30 April 4
John 19:25–27 May 29
John 19:38–42 April 5
John 19:41–20:18 December 30
John 20:19–20 April 14
John 21:4–14 July 21

Acts 2:44–45 June 11
Acts 2:44–47 April 9, November 6
Acts 3:1–10 August 6, November 15
Acts 6:2–7 July 27
Acts 8:5–8 October 5
Acts 8:26–31 July 23
Acts 9:23–25 November 23
Acts 9:26–28 April 17
Acts 9:36–42 September 5
Acts 15:22–23 March 25
Acts 16:11–15 February 8
Acts 18:1–3 March 11
Acts 27:21–26, 33–38, 43–44 February 13
Acts 27:27–44 March 30

Romans 16:1–2 November 7

1 Corinthians 13:4–8 May 8
1 Corinthians 16:14 July 16

2 Corinthians 1:3–4 January 7, February 29

Galatians 5:22–23 January 17

Ephesians 4:2–3 March 4
Ephesians 4:29 January 26
Ephesians 4:31–32 April 30
Ephesians 4:32 August 29
Ephesians 6:1 April 15
Ephesians 6:1–3 January 20, June 6
Ephesians 6:13–17 February 15

Philippians 1:3–8 March 17
Philippians 2:4 June 29
Philippians 4:2–5 May 16
Philippians 4:4 September 21
Philippians 4:8 February 23

Colossians 3:12–14 April 23
Colossians 3:13 October 16
Colossians 3:20 May 11
Colossians 3:20, 23 March 19
Colossians 4:7–14 June 16

1 Thessalonians 5:15 October 3

2 Timothy 3:16–17 January 11
2 Timothy 4:13 March 6

Hebrews 10:24 January 25
Hebrews 12:1–3 April 2
Hebrews 13:5 January 30

James 5:7–8 August 31

1 Peter 5:7 October 18

1 John 1:9 August 28
1 John 4:21 July 31
1 John 5:2–3 August 13

Revelation 21:3–4 December 18